HORIZON

MARCH, 1962 · VOLUME IV, NUMBER 4

HORIZON
A Magazine of the Arts

MARCH, 1962 · VOLUME IV, NUMBER 4

PUBLISHER
James Parton

EDITORIAL DIRECTOR
Joseph J. Thorndike, Jr.

EDITOR
William Harlan Hale
MANAGING EDITOR
Eric Larrabee
ASSOCIATE EDITOR
Ralph Backlund
ASSISTANT EDITORS
Ada Pesin
Jane Wilson
Albert Bermel
CONTRIBUTING EDITOR
Margery Darrell
EDITORIAL ASSISTANTS
Shirley Abbott, Caroline Backlund
Wendy Buehr, Alan Doré, Charles L. Mee, Jr.
COPY EDITOR
Mary Ann Pfeiffer
Assistants: Joan Rehe, Ruth H. Wolfe

ART DIRECTOR
Irwin Glusker
Associate Art Director: Elton Robinson

ADVISORY BOARD
Gilbert Highet, Chairman
Frederick Burkhardt   Oliver Jensen
Marshall B. Davidson   Jotham Johnson
Richard M. Ketchum   John Walker

EUROPEAN CONSULTING EDITOR
J. H. Plumb
Christ's College, Cambridge

EUROPEAN BUREAU
Gertrudis Feliu, Chief
28 Quai du Louvre, Paris

HORIZON is published every two months by American Heritage Publishing Co., Inc. Executive and editorial offices: 551 Fifth Ave., New York 17, N.Y. HORIZON welcomes contributions but can assume no responsibility for unsolicited material.

All correspondence about subscriptions should be addressed to: HORIZON Subscription Office, 379 West Center St., Marion, Ohio.

Single Copies: $4.50
Annual Subscriptions: $21.00 in the U.S. & Can.
$22.00 elsewhere

An annual index is published every September, priced at $1. HORIZON is also indexed in the Readers Guide to Periodical Literature.

Title registered U.S. Patent Office
Second-class postage paid at New York, N.Y.

COVER: Against a background of the glowing crimson that has since come to be known as "Pompeian red," a trembling woman waits for the blows of a lash. This is no scene from the Marquis de Sade, nor even from Uncle Tom's Cabin, but a detail from one of the frescoes uncovered at Pompeii. It reveals a little about pagan religious cults and a great deal more about the high state of painting in that luxurious Roman colony before it was buried in A.D. 79. An article about the rediscovery of Pompeii and Herculaneum in the eighteenth century, and its effect on taste ever since, begins on page 42.

FRONTISPIECE: At least seven hundred years before the Incas put their more familiar stamp on Andean civilization, the Mochica people of Peru's northern coast were producing such sophisticated work as this kingfisher of cast copper inlaid with fragments of shell. It was probably the head of a ceremonial staff—perhaps the badge of office of some chieftain—and was made sometime between A.D. 600 and 800. Centuries of oxidation have replaced its once coppery gleam with a brilliant green patina. This rara avis from the collection of Raymond Wielgus of Chicago was part of an exhibition of the arts of Peru at the American Museum of Natural History in New York last winter.

THE TIME OF MAN

Once he was thought a fallen angel; then we found him to be a descended ape. Today, new finds are revolutionizing our ideas about his origins and the growth of that unique great brain which he may yet put to fatal use

It is a curious thought that as I sit down to write this essay on the history of our species, I do so in the heightened consciousness that it may never be published: a holocaust may overtake it. Tomorrow I may lie under tons of rubble, precipitated into the street along with the paper on which this history is scribbled. Over the whole earth—this infinitely small globe that possesses all we know of sunshine and bird song—an unfamiliar blight is creeping: man—man, who has become at last a planetary disease and who would, if his technology yet permitted, pass this infection to another star. If I write this history in brief compass it is because, on the scale of the universe, it is but an instant, shot with individual glory and unimaginable shame. Man is the only infinitely corruptible as well as infinitely perfectible animal.

The story I here record contains many gaps and few names. Most of what has gone into the making of man is as nameless as the nothing from which he sprang and into which, by his own hand, he threatens to subside. He has wandered unclothed through earth's long interglacial summers; he has huddled before fires in equally millennial winters. He has mated and fought for a bare existence like earth's other creatures. Unlike these others, however, he has clothed his dreams in magic that slowly became science—the science that was to bring him all things. And so, because of the dark twist in his mind, it has; it has brought him even unto death.

This story, then, is written in a kind of fatal haste—to

be read by whom, I wonder? Or does it matter? Man is the talking animal. I shall talk to myself if necessary. I feel my own face before the mirror, touch the risen brain vault over the gray layer of cells that has brought us to this destiny. I lift up my hands under the light. There is no fur, black upon them, any longer.

For a moment I wish there were—for a moment of desperate terror I wish to hurtle backward like a scuttling crab into my evolutionary shell, to be swinging ape and leaping Tupaiid; yes, or sleeping reptile on a stream bank—anything but the thing I have become. He who enters history encounters burdens he cannot bear, and traps more subtle than his subtlest thought. No one quite knows how man became concerned with this torrent called history. He contrives it out of his own substance and then calls it an "act of God" when the tanks grind forward over his own body.

A strange animal, indeed: so very quiet when one turns over the mineral-hardened skull in a gravel bed, or peers into that little dark space which has housed so much cruelty and delight. One feels that something should be there still, some indefinable essence, some jinni to be evoked out of this little space which may contain at the same time the words of Jesus and the blasphemous megatons of modern physics. They are all in there together, inextricably intermixed, and this is how the mixture began.

There are innumerable detailed questions of dating and of detailed anatomical analysis and interpretation of those scant human remains which through gaps of hundreds of

By LOREN EISELEY

thousands, even of millions of years, enable us to secure brief glimpses of our nameless forerunners. For a hundred years—ever since the theory of evolution became biologically demonstrable—these facts have been accumulating. To catalogue them, to debate their several arguments, would require volumes. It is my intention in this article merely to select for discussion a few key items which continue to intrigue the educated layman, and which may help him to comprehend not alone a few of the mileposts of his long journey but which may give him as well a better comprehension of his own nature and the built-in dangers it contains. The moment is topical, for it is within the past year that discoveries have been made which may drastically change our ideas about our earliest past.

We will begin with a warning: more than 90 per cent of the world's animal life of past periods is dead. Though it flourished in some instances longer than the whole period of human development, somewhere along its evolutionary path one of two things happened. It vanished without descendants or was transformed, through still mysterious biological processes, into something else; just as man is now something quite different from what he was ten million years ago. This leads to the inescapable conclusion that, contrary to popular impression, evolution is not something "behind" us—the impression we may get while staring into museum cases.

So long as life exists on the planet, it is still changing, adjusting, and vanishing as natural forces—and among them we must now count man—may dictate. Thus life is never really perfectly adjusted. It is malleable and imperfect because it is always slipping from one world into another. The perfectly adjusted perish with the environments that created them. It is not really surprising, when one thinks about it, that man, who evolved with comparative rapidity, should be among earth's most dangerous juvenile delinquents.

He is literally compounded of contradictions, mentally and physically. He is at one and the same time archaic and advanced. His body and his mind are as stuffed with evolutionary refuse as a New England attic. Once he comes to accept and recognize this fact, his chances for survival may improve. He has come halfway on a trembling bridge toward heaven, but the human brain in its loss of life-preserving instincts passes also along the brink of sanity. Here is a great poet, John Donne, speaking three centuries ago of the power of the human intellect:

Inlarge this Meditation upon this great world, Man, so farr, as to consider the immensitie of the creatures this world produces: our creatures are our thoughts, creatures that are borne Gyants; that reach from East to West, from Earth to Heaven, that doe not onely bestride all the Sea, and Land, but span the Sunn and Firmament at once; My thoughts reach all, comprehend all. Inexplicable mistery; I their Creator am in a close prison, in a sicke bed, any where, and any one of my Creatures, my thoughts, is with the Sunne, and beyond the Sunne, overtakes the Sunne, and overgoes the Sunne in one pace, one steppe, everywhere.

Man, in short, has, like no other beast, tumbled into the crevasse of his own being, fallen into the deep well of his own mind. Like modern divers in the sacrificial wells of the Maya, he has drawn from his own depths such vast edifices as the Pyramids, or inscribed on cave walls the animals of his primitive environment, fixed by a magic that inhabited his mind. He retreats within and he appears outward. Even the fallen temples of his dead endeavors affect, like strange symbols, the minds of later-comers. There is something immaterial that haunts the air, something other than the life force in squirrel and chipmunk. Here, even in ruin, something drawn from the depths of our being may speak a message across the waste of centuries.

A little while ago I handled a flint knife, from Stone Age Egypt, running my hand over its beautifully rippled surface. A human mind, an artist's mind, whispered to me from the stone. I held the knife a long time, just as in another way I might hold in my mind the sunlit Parthenon, feeling some emanation, some re-entering power deriving from minds long past but flooding my own thought with renewed powers and novelties. This is a part, a mystical part if you will, of man's emergence into time and history.

When he entered into himself, as no other animal on the globe is capable of doing, he also entered the strangest environmental corridor on the planet, one almost infinite in its possibilities, its terrors, and its hopes. It was the world of history, of symbolic thought, of culture. From the moment when the human brain, even in its dim red morning, crossed that threshold, it would never again be satisfied with the things of earth. It would heft a stone and make of it a tool grown from the mind; fire would become its instrument; sails on the invisible air would waft it far; eventually a little needle in a box would guide men to new continents and polar snows. In each case there would also be the aura of magic. The powers would not be what we of today call natural; around them would hover a penumbral mystery drawn from the abysses of the mind itself. Time and the foreknowledge of death would rise also in that spectral light. Of the fears that beset our dawning consciousness, the brown bone on the shores of a vanished lake bed will tell us nothing. It will tell us only how we changed.

From whence did we come? Over and over again the scholar is asked this question by those who forget the wounds and changes in the bone. Do they ask upon which continent we first stood dubiously erect? Do they ask from what limb in an ancient forest we first hung and by some idle quirk dropped down into the long grass that first received us? Do they want to know at what point we first asked a question of some wandering constellation in the night sky above our heads? Or from what marsh we first dragged our wet amphibian bodies up the shore? Or from what reptilian egg we sprang? Or from what cell in some far, steaming sea?

No, the question has to be contained and caught within the primate order to which we and all manner of ring-tailed, wide-eyed lemurs, blue-chinned monkeys, and enormous apes belong. With these we share certain facets of a common bodily structure that speaks of ancient relationships. In a strange, figurative way there was a time far back along the evolutionary road when all this weird array might be seen to shrink to a single tree shrew, a single ratty insectivore upon a branch. Man, at that moment, was one of many potentials. He was and was not, and likewise all his hairy and fantastic kin. They all quivered there upon that single branch in one frail body—Socrates, Confucius, and Gargantua, along with the organ-grinder's monkey.

The student asks you, as a child his mother, "Where did I come from?" "Son," you say floundering, "below the Cambrian there was a worm." Or you say, "There was an odd fish in a swamp and you have his lungs." Or you say, "Once there was a reptile whose jaw bones are in your ear." Or you try again. "There was an ape and his teeth are in your mouth. Your jaw has shrunk and your skull has risen. You are fish and reptile and a warm-blooded, affectionate thing that dies if it has nothing to cling to when it is young. You are all of these things. You are also a rag doll made of patches out of many ages and skins. You began nowhere in particular. You are really an illusion, one of innumerable shadows in the dying fires of a mysterious universe. Yesterday you were a lowbrowed skull in the river gravel; tomorrow you may be a fleck of carbon amid the shattered glass of Moscow or New York. Ninety per cent of the world's life has already gone. Perhaps brains will accomplish the work of extinction faster. The pace is stepping up."

"Life," a cynical philosopher once shrewdly observed, "is a supremely illogical business. One can become dark from excess of light." This statement is so directly applicable to the study of human evolution that it ought to preface any survey of our past. At first glance everything is simple. We have a bone here, a skull there. Teeth grow smaller, brains grow larger. The upright posture undoubtedly preceded by perhaps a million years or more the appearance of a face and brain faintly comparable to our own.

Even after the brain began to grow, it was long shielded by a shell of bone as thick as a warrior's helmet. It was as if nature itself was dubious of the survival of this strange instrument, yet had taken steps to protect it. I like to think that with the invention of a brain capable of symbolic thought—and, as an unsought corollary, philosophy— something behind nature rejoiced to look out upon itself. That massively walled brain, even in its early beginnings, had taken life three billion years to produce. But the future of no invention can be guaranteed. As in the case of other forms of life in the past, extinction may come about some millennia hence from "natural" causes. Or—as we are constantly reminded by our experts—life's most dazzling invention may, through the employment of its own wizardry,

MAN'S FAMILY TREE: 1962 VERSION

Recent discoveries have thrown new light upon man's evolutionary history, but "only the dim light of morning," in Loren Eiseley's phrase, so far illumines our knowledge of human origins. The chart opposite reflects today's complex view of primate evolution, in contrast to the straight-line concept of a century ago (see insert). Various living primates—survivors of a process of some sixty million years during which most forms vanished—are shown at the top in typical postures. The heavy lines ascending to them are diagrammatic only, taking the place of myriad untraceable networks of intersecting, converging, and parallel lines (suggested by the lighter strokes). Glacial periods are indicated in blue; the deepening browns of remoter geological epochs are a reminder that these are not drawn to scale.

A hundred years ago, scientists—working with only living forms and a single fossil, the Neanderthal skull, as evidence—thought modern man had descended directly from the apes by way of Neanderthal man (as the traditional "family tree" at lower right indicates). But as more fossils have been found and studied, this conception has changed radically. It is now known that man clearly could not have evolved from any present-day species; rather, both he and the apes must have evolved independently from some rudimentary common ancestor, now extinct.

A primitive ape from the Miocene epoch, Proconsul, *may have been such a forerunner. A later creature,* Oreopithecus, *found in the coal fields of Tuscany, may have been close to the early human line. The next fossil in ascending order on the chart,* Zinjanthropus, *was discovered only in 1959; he appears to be one of the slender, erect-walking man-apes called* Australopithecines, *whose skeletons and teeth show stronger resemblances to man than to apes. Their brain was apelike in size, but the fact that shaped stone implements were found alongside* Zinjanthropus *indicates he was a toolmaker—that is, a man. Last July he was dated by a new radioactive-decay process at the astonishing age of nearly two million years, three times the estimate for other Australopithecines. If this date proves correct, man will be known to have emerged much earlier than has been thought.*

Java and Peking men are evolutionary brothers, similar to each other and, except for their massive skulls and small brains, to ourselves. The classic Neanderthals, or "cave men," however, now seem to have reached an evolutionary dead end in the late Pleistocene; some Neanderthals may have contributed genetically to Homo sapiens, *but the type is no longer considered our direct forerunner. Indeed, before human evolution can be traced with any certainty, still unknown forms of man or pre-man, particularly from the long, dark Pliocene epoch, must be unearthed.* Zinjanthropus *may be a harbinger of just such discoveries.*

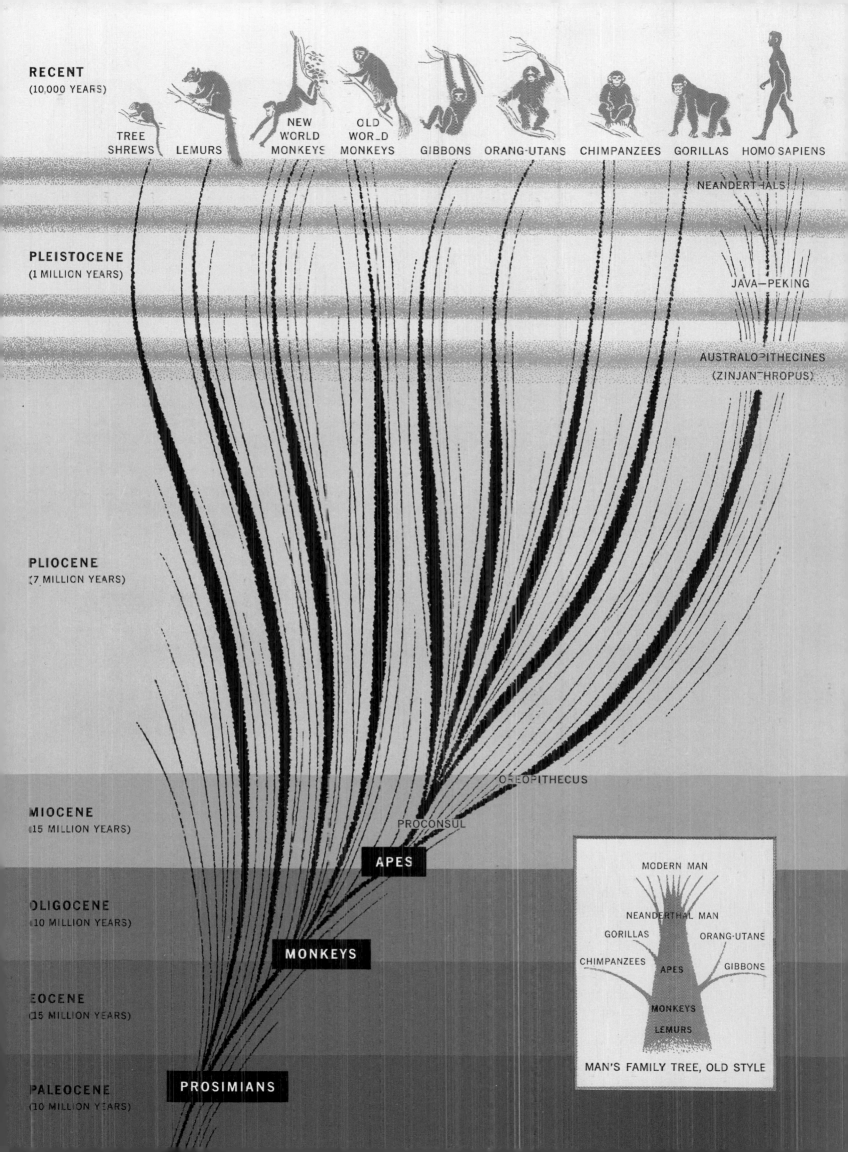

RECENT
(10,000 YEARS)

TREE SHREWS LEMURS NEW WORLD MONKEYS OLD WORLD MONKEYS GIBBONS ORANG-UTANS CHIMPANZEES GORILLAS HOMO SAPIENS

NEANDERTHALS

PLEISTOCENE
(1 MILLION YEARS)

JAVA–PEKING

AUSTRALOPITHECINES
(ZINJANTHROPUS)

PLIOCENE
(7 MILLION YEARS)

OREOPITHECUS

MIOCENE
(15 MILLION YEARS)

PROCONSUL

APES

OLIGOCENE
(10 MILLION YEARS)

MONKEYS

EOCENE
(15 MILLION YEARS)

PALEOCENE
(10 MILLION YEARS)

PROSIMIANS

MODERN MAN

NEANDERTHAL MAN

GORILLAS   ORANG-UTANS

CHIMPANZEES   GIBBONS

APES

MONKEYS

LEMURS

MAN'S FAMILY TREE, OLD STYLE

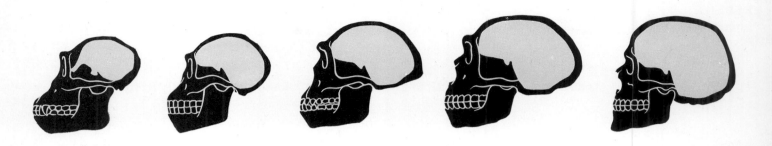

Man has become man through a phenomenal growth of the primate brain, chiefly in the frontal areas that control memory and speech. But while these diagrams compare the skulls of a present-day ape (left) and Homo sapiens *(right) with* *fossils in between (in sequence,* Australopithecus, *Peking, and Neanderthal man), mystery surrounds our direct lines of ancestry and the rise of what Dr. Eiseley calls this "strange instrument"—the gray matter that is our ultimate weapon.*

soon be able to erase itself completely from the earth, in a matter not of millennia, but of minutes.

For the human brain, magnificent though it be, is as yet imperfect and bears within itself an old and lower brain—a fossil remnant, one might say—geared to the existence of a creature struggling to become human, and dragged with him, unfortunately, out of the Ice Age. This ancient brain, capable of violent and dominant re-emergence under various conditions of stress, contains, figuratively speaking, claws— claws which by now can be fantastically extended.

Life *is* illogical, and if one looks long and steadily at evolution and at man in particular, the illumination provided by fossil skulls can produce, paradoxically, some profound shadows. In the early history of anthropological studies, when we possessed few human remains but much acquaintance with our living relatives in the trees, the story had seemed simpler: somewhere, not too far back in time, an ape had gotten down from his tree, driven to the ground, possibly, by a growing desiccation of the landscape. In time natural selection had altered an arboreal foot for bipedal progression, and the hands, once used by our ancestors for the manipulation of the branches among which they dwelt, were now employed in the exploration and eventual remaking of the world into which they had intruded. There is, indeed, a certain semblance of truth in this account, but with every discovery of the past few decades, the story has had to be modified if not rewritten. Even today, while no reasonable man doubts the reality of human evolution, its precise pathways are hazy, and far gaps in time and space make the exact succession of forms difficult if not impossible to determine.

It is easy when bones are few, to stick to a single line of ascent or to give a simple version of events (see insert chart, "Man's Family Tree, Old Style," page 7). But bones also have their limitations. We cannot trace the living races far into the past. We know little or nothing about why man lost his fur. Consider the mistakes to which our descendants, a million years forward in time, would be liable in trying to reconstruct, without a single written document, the events of

today. To tell the truth, though theories abound, we know little about why man became man at all.

We know as much—and as little—about our own ancestors as we do about some other missing creatures from the geological record. Why, for example, do bats hurl themselves so suddenly upon us, fully formed, out of the Paleocene era? They emerge with comparative rapidity in the dawn of mammalian history. In fact they bear a distant relationship to ourselves. How they became bats and not men is one of those evolutionary problems which involve the interplay of vast and ill-understood forces operating over enormous lengths of time.

The light being thrown upon our history is truly only the dim light of morning. I often think, on taking off my shoes at night, that they clothe an awkward and still imperfect evolutionary instrument. Our feet are easily sprained or injured, and somehow comical. If they had not been reshaped in some long venture on the early grasslands, we would not find it so satisfactory now to brace them artificially in shoes. The sight of them is chastening to pride. The little toe is attractive to the student of rudimentary and vanishing organs; the over-all perspective is a rude palimpsest, a scratched-out and rewritten autobiography whose first anatomical pages were contrived in some arboreal attic.

Among these living shards and remnants of the past, however, it is easy to linger and be lost. I remarked that we know little about why it was necessary to become man at all. There are many parallelisms in the other parts of nature. Complex social life has arisen several times in diverse insect orders. There are flying marsupials as well as flying placental mammals. But man, the thinker, has occurred but once in the three billion years that may be the length of life's endurance on this planet.

He is an inconceivably rare and strange beast who lives both within himself and in his outside environment. With his coming came history, the art of the mind imposing itself upon nature. There has been no previous evolutionary novelty comparable to this save the act of creation itself. Man, imperfect transitory man, carries within him some uncanny spark from the first lightning that split the void. He alone can dilate evil by drawing upon the innocent powers contained in nature; he alone can walk straight-footed to his own death and hold the world well lost for the sake of such intangible things as truth and love.

Yet let me suggest once more that we look long and clearly at ourselves, our strange and naked bodies, our evolutionary wounds, wracked as we have been through trees and lion-haunted grasslands and by the growing failure of instinct to guide us well. Let us take care, for beyond this point in time, brains and sympathy—the mark of our humanity—will alone have to guide us. The precedent of the forest will be wrong, the precedent of our dark and violent mid-brains will be wrong; everything, in short, will be wrong but compassion—and we are still the two-fold beast. Why did we have to be man, we ask ourselves, as the Christians of another day must have asked: "How can man be made whole? How can he be restored to the innocence he knew before the Fall?"

In one of those great insights that embellish the work of the stylist and philosopher George Santayana, he wrote sadly: "The Universe is the true Adam, the Creation the true Fall." He saw, that wise old man who has left us, that to come out of the blessed dark of nonbeing, to endure time and the disturbances of matter, is to be always subject to the unexpected even if it masquerades as "natural law." With the unexpected comes evil, the unforeseen, the moment's weakness. Life—even nonhuman life—becomes parasitic, devours its fellows, until a Darwin looking on may call it "devil's work." The creation falls and falls again. In mortal time, in Santayana's sense, it must ever fall. Yet the falling brings not only strange, dark, and unexpected ends to innocent creatures but also death to tyrannous monsters.

The very novelties of life offer renewed hope to the spirit that works upon intransigent matter and lends us our willingness to endure our time. For us, for this little day we inhabit so unthinkingly, much has been suffered. A gray and shadowy and bestial thing had to become a man. Gleams, strange lights, half-caught visions of both love and abominable terror, must have dogged our footsteps. Disease destroyed us in infancy. We were abruptly orphaned, and great teeth struck us down. We were fearful of the dead who haunted our dreams. We barked and gabbled until, at some unknown point in time, the first meaningful inverted sounds in all the world were heard in some lost meadow. The creature had stumbled, with the growth of speech, into a vast interior world. Soon it would dominate his outer world.

A year ago most of us who work in this haunted graveyard of the past would have said that a brain which we could truly denominate as human was perhaps no older than the lower Ice Age, and that below the million years or so of Ice Age time, man, even lowbrowed, thick-skulled man, had vanished from our ken. If, that far back, he still walked, he was not a tool-user; if he still talked, his thoughts had found no lasting expression upon the objects of his outer world. It appeared to us not that he had vanished in the seven-million-year epoch of the Pliocene, but rather that he was a thinly distributed ground ape, a late descendant upon the upland grasses, still teetering upon a dubiously adapted foot from one sparse clump of trees to another.

In July, 1961, our ideas were destined to change drastically. They were to change not so much because of a newly described form of early man from Africa—we had grown used to that—but rather because of what a new method of dating was to tell us about humanity in general.

Over the previous thirty years a startling series of discoveries in South and East Africa had revealed that the simplified versions of single-line human evolution were very unlikely to be true. It was soon realized that African humanity has a very ancient history—more ancient than, at present, we can demonstrate for any other part of Asia or Europe. I am not now speaking of problematic early relatives of ours such as *Oreopithecus* from the Tuscan coal mines of Italy, but of tool-using creatures walking upon the ground.

Deep in the Olduvai Gorge in Kenya lay hand axes of enormous antiquity. Even more primitive pebble tools were found in various regions in South Africa. Man—some kind of heavy-browed man—had long roved the uplands of that game-filled continent. Darwin's guess that Africa might prove to be the original home of man was taking on renewed interest, even though very ancient remains such as Peking Man had been located in the caves of Choukoutien, and a series of early forms had also turned up in Java. It must be remembered also that the inhospitable desert break between Africa and southwestern Asia has not always existed. In early ages it is likely that freedom of movement between these two regions was far more simple for primitive man and beast than has been true in historic times. Hence, since so much of Asia remains archaeologically unknown, it would be premature to decide that Africa alone contains the full story of the human past. That it has provided us with more clues to early human development than any other region, however, it would now be idle to deny.

All through the past few decades the labors of such pioneer scients as Robert Broom, Raymond Dart, L. S. B. Leakey, and J. T. Robinson have succeeded in turning up amid the breccia of ancient cave deposits a hitherto totally unsuspected and apparently cultureless group of ape-men, or perhaps one should say man-apes. Instead of gorilloid, long-fanged creatures lately descended from the trees, such as the early Darwinists would have envisaged, these creatures, of whom numerous remains and several species have been recovered, brought dramatically home to us a largely unsuspected aspect of the human story, anticipated on theoretical grounds only by Darwin's great contemporary Alfred Russel Wallace.

The idea of the gorilloid nature of early man as advanced

by many nineteenth-century scientists was not borne out by the new-found fossils. Instead, the bones proved to be those of rather slightly built, erect-walking "apes" with massive molar teeth unaccompanied by projecting canines. In short, the animals turned out to be a rather variable lot of short-faced, small-brained creatures already adapted for walking on their hind feet. Long arguments developed as to whether these creatures of some 500 cubic centimeters of cranial capacity—roughly akin to the brain size of a modern chimpanzee or gorilla—could have made crude tools, or at least utilized the long bones of slain animals as clubs or stabbing weapons. This was possible—but difficult to prove.

One thing, at least, had become evident. The man-apes represented not recently arboreal apes but, instead, an unsuspected variety of erect-walking anthropoids whose foot adaptation to a ground-dwelling existence was already greatly perfected. In Tertiary times large primates had not been confined to the trees. Instead, they had successfully brought their old-fashioned arboreal bodies down onto the grass and survived there—a feat of no mean magnitude. By some evolutionary neurological quirk they had acquired an upright posture which had freed the forelimbs from the demands of locomotion. Man bears in his body clear signs of an early apprenticeship in the trees. We now began to suspect, however, that man had served his arboreal apprenticeship much farther back in time than many scholars had anticipated. It also became evident that the number of forms and datings of what soon came to be called the Australopithecine man-apes could only suggest that not all of them were direct human ancestors. These African creatures hinted rather of a variety of early man-apes, not all of whom had necessarily taken the final step of becoming human.

A group of apes had entered upon a new way of life in open park land and grassland. Arboreal apes are not carnivorous; they are primarily vegetarians. But these man-apes, or perhaps I should say *some* of these man-apes, had become killers of game. Their massive jaws, however, are not evidence of this fact. Massive molar teeth may mean only the consumption of certain types of uncooked vegetation. It is the broken bones of animals in the caves they frequented which suggest that some species, at least, had become killers, using their unloosed forelimbs as weapon wielders.* As for the brain, perhaps though still small, the upright posture had given this organ some qualitative advantage over the brains of our living relatives, the great apes.

Still, we had to look upon these creatures as essentially an odd, humanlike ape. Like any other animal, they had intruded into and adapted themselves to a grassland existence; it seems unlikely that they could speak. It appears unlikely, also, that all these creatures survived to become men; some may have been living fossils in their own time. The last of them may have been exterminated by the spread of man himself. But they indicate that the bipedal apes were well

adapted to survive upon the ground without entering extensively upon a second road of conquest.

It remained for the direct human ancestors, from whatever bipedal group they may have sprung, to precipitate the final stage in man's development: the rise of the great brain, still marked by its ferocious past. For man entered, with the development of speech and its ever-growing product, culture, into the strangest and most rapidly changing environment on the planet, an environment limited only by his own creativeness. He entered into himself; he created society and its institutions. The exterior, natural world would be modified and pushed farther and farther back by the magic circle in which he had immured himself. Some societies would dream on for millennia in a world still close to nature; other roads would lead to the Greek thinkers and the Roman aqueducts. The history of the world-changers had begun.

We can still ask of this varied group of fossils, why did man have to be? No answer comes back. He did not have to be any more than a butterfly or a caterpillar. He merely emerged from that infinite void for which we have no name.

In 1959 Dr. L. S. B. Leakey found at Olduvai the massive-jawed, small-brained creature who has come to be known as *Zinjanthropus*. Though detailed anatomical data are not available, the creature would appear to be not too distant in its anatomy from some of the known, and possibly much later, man-apes. It, however, is remarkable for two reasons. First, it was found in association with clearly shaped stone tools, long known but never found in direct contact with human remains. Thus this creature was not merely a user of chance things which he picked up; he was a thinker who shaped. Second, late last July Doctors J. F. Evenden and Garniss Curtis of the University of California announced that *Zinjanthropus* was nearly *two* million years old. They had dated the creature by a new "clock" involving the use of potassium-argon radioactive decay. If this dating method is correct, the history of tool-using man will thus have been carried back almost a million years before the Ice Age—and Dr. Leakey has reported an even earlier find, as yet undescribed, from the same vicinity.

Previously I have mentioned that man's mental development, so far as its later, bigger-brained phase is concerned, has seemed rapid. Dr. Leakey's find can be interpreted in two ways: as suggesting that the incipient steps leading to the emergence of the large brain began earlier than we have anticipated, or that man drifted in a static fashion on this simple level for a long period before some new mutation or latent dynamism generated a new leap forward in brain size. Little in the way of advanced cultural remains is known before the later Pleistocene, so that the appearance of this tool-using creature of such archaic countenance is an amazingly disturbing element to our thinking.

Have all our lower Ice Age discoveries been underestimated as to time? And what of the other, the seemingly later yet more primitive Australopithecines? Are they, then, true

---

* See Robert Ardrey's commentary on the implications of these finds, "How Can Man Get Along Without War," HORIZON, November, 1961.

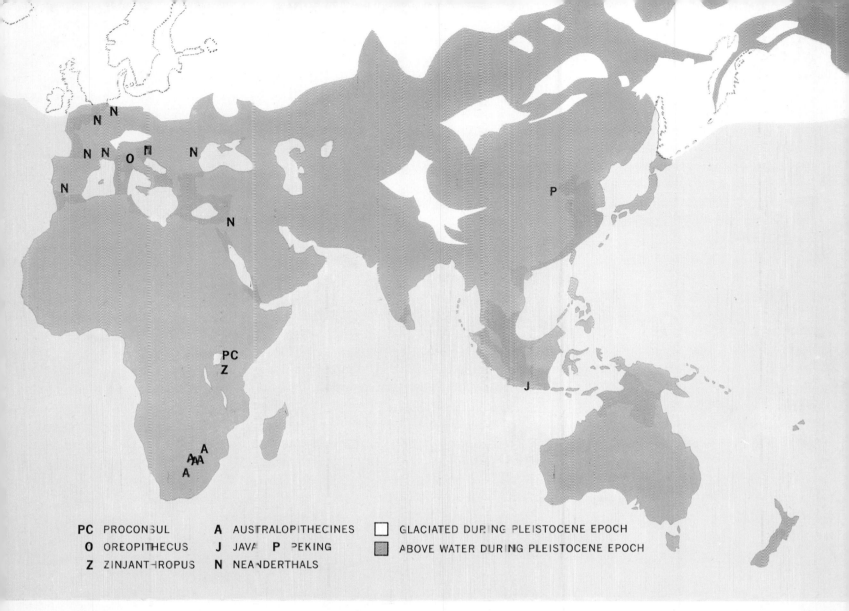

PC PROCONSUL   A AUSTRALOPITHECINES   ☐ GLACIATED DURING PLEISTOCENE EPOCH

O OREOPITHECUS   J JAVA   P PEKING   ▨ ABOVE WATER DURING PLEISTOCENE EPOCH

Z ZINJANTHROPUS   N NEANDERTHALS

Where did man begin? Anthropological science, starting in Europe, found its first fossils (the Neanderthals) near home. Then came the discoveries of Java and Peking men. In our generation, finds of great antiquity in Africa (the Australopithecines and Zinjanthropus) have lent new interest to Darwin's guess that Africa might be our ancestral home. Glacial periods, by lowering sea levels and linking Africa and Java to the Eurasian continent, may have aided man's spread.

cousins rather than ancestors—survivals of an even more remote past? We do not know. We know only that darkest Africa is not dark by reason of its present history alone. Contained in that vast continent may be the secret of our origin and the secret of the rise of that dread organ which has unlocked the wild powers of the universe and yet taught us all we know of compassion and of love.

Those ancient bestial stirrings which still claw at sanity are part, also, of that dark continent we long chose to forget. But we do not forget, because man in contemplation reveals something that is characteristic of no other form of life known to us: he suffers because of what he is, and wishes to become something else. The moment we cease to hunger to be otherwise, our soul is dead. Long ago we began that hunger; long ago we painted on the walls of caverns and buried the revered dead. More and more, because our brain lays hold upon and seeks to shape the future, we are conscious of what we are, and what we might be. "No man," wrote John Donne, "doth exalt Nature to the height it would beare." He saw the discrepancy between dream and reality.

Great minds have always seen it. That is why man has survived his journey this long. When we fail to wish any longer to be otherwise than what we are, we will have ceased to evolve. Evolution has to be lived forward. I say this as one who has stood above the bones of much that has vanished, and at midnight have examined my own face.

Prized as a student and writer in his field of the science of man, Dr. Eiseley is the author of Darwin's Century *and* The Firmament of Time *(the final chapter of which first appeared in* HORIZON, *July, 1960). Long the Provost of the University of Pennsylvania, he is soon to become its University Professor of Anthropology and the History of Science.*

In his latest incarnation Edmund Kean was impersonated by Alfred Drake in the title role of Kean, *the Broadway musical based on a Sartre play which was in turn based on a play of Dumas* père *about the actor's stormy life. The scene at right had one of his loves, the Countess de Koeberg (Joan Weldon), sharing his drawing room and a duet. The romantic partners of the real Kean (opposite page, costumed as Hamlet) did not include titled ladies.*

The Trail of the
SPLENDID GYPSY

Edmund Kean's "natural" acting won

the applause of Keats, Shelley, Byron, and Coleridge,

but it was his melodramatic life that inspired

a succession of plays, and finally a Broadway musical

In Shakespeare's *Twelfth Night* one of the minor characters remarks, "If this were played upon a stage now, I could condemn it as an improbable fiction." The line might serve as an epigraph to the phenomenon of the actor Edmund Kean, a prodigious Englishman whose private life was as theatrical as his public career. Kean could be said to have originated the type of the tortured, flamboyant actor, becoming in the eyes of his generation and those that followed it an epitome of romanticism. He first appeared on the American stage in 1820, and he came back to it again in 1961, as the central figure in a lavish musical named after him. In the intervening century his life has served as the material for a number of dramatists, even though some of them—like Alexandre Dumas and Jean-Paul Sartre—felt it necessary to alter

details for the sake of credibility. Art, after all, insists on certain restraints that do not hamper reality.

Edmund Kean was the illegitimate son of a London actress-*cum*-harlot named Ann Carey, granddaughter of that Henry Carey who, some claim, was the author of "God Save the King." Kean's birth date is often given as November 4, 1787, but as Giles Playfair points out in his excellent biography, a more likely date is March 17, 1790. Charlotte Tidswell, the remarkable woman who helped to rear the boy, remembered that she was summoned to the mother's childbed on a St. Patrick's Day; and a playbill of the year 1801 refers to Kean as "The Celebrated Theatrical Child . . . not eleven years old." His father, also named Edmund Kean, was a surveyor's apprentice who committed

CONTINUED ON PAGE 114

By STANLEY KAUFFMANN

13

The Simple Seer

A modest man
with joyous daydreams,
Pierre Bonnard created
an enchanted land
where all is light

By PIERRE SCHNEIDER

The artist (in 1944) stands before one of his paintings. Many later became the subject of a bizarre lawsuit

In the Museum of Modern Art in Paris there hangs a picture before which visitors seldom pause—and right they are, for it is one of the most boring: Maurice Denis's *Homage to Cézanne*. Around the master beside his easel, a group stands frozen in admiration. They are artists, a critic, an art dealer, uniformly dignified, looking serious and middle-aged. One man, however, strikes an off note in this solemn gathering. As if to indicate his difference, he is placed somewhat apart from the others. He has the air of a schoolboy too big for his clothes who has wandered inadvertently into a meeting of the board of directors. At once detached and attentive, he seems not quite there, lost in a reverie yet on his good behavior. His myopic eyes are hidden behind round, owlish glasses, and an apologetic smile plays about his lips. Shyness radiates from the tall, narrow-shouldered figure clad with almost conspicuous inconspicuousness. There can't be the slightest doubt as to the identity of this long face with the slightly receding chin: there, in all his bank-clerkish propriety, stands Walter Mitty. With one capital difference, however: a miracle has brought *this* Mr. Mitty's private world into the public domain so all may be enchanted by its cloudless fantasy. For the timid fellow's name is Pierre Bonnard.

At first, his life (1867–1947) conforms strictly to the Mittyish line. He was born at Fontenay-aux-Roses, a suburb of Paris; his father headed a department at the Ministry of War, and Pierre was given the careful secondary education which leads obedient sons to a secure job in the civil service. He successfully passed his baccalaureate examinations and even obtained a diploma in law, although here the first disquieting signs of deviation appeared: back home after his day of study, he frequently sketched the faces of people seen in the Metro, on his way to and from the University. The signs grew more ominous when he failed his civil service exam: had he passed it, he might have spent his life checking records and statistics. And the scandal broke when the judge who had hired him as a clerk, intrigued by the unusual zeal with which he buried himself beneath mountains of legal files, found him drawing and promptly fired him. By then, Bonnard's mind was made up: he would be a painter. But it was not until his poster for a champagne company gaily splashed the walls of Paris, in 1891, that his father gave in. What motivated Bonnard *père* to do so was not that Toulouse-Lautrec liked the poster so much that he asked to meet its young author, but the fact that Pierre had been paid all of 100 francs for it.

Actually, Bonnard had been painting for several years. After attending courses at the Ecole des Beaux-Arts and competing—again, praise heaven, unsuccessfully—for the Prix de Rome (an award given annually to a studious, white-collar worker of the brush and easel), he continued his apprenticeship at the Académie Jullian. Instruction there was not any more revolutionary than at the Beaux-Arts, but Bonnard met a handful of contemporaries who were soon to become close friends: Paul Sérusier, Paul Ranson, Maurice Denis, Ker-Xavier Roussel, Edouard Vuillard. Still ignorant of the bright universe discovered by the impressionists, they worked ploddingly in the dark, naturalistic style then fashionable, until the day, in 1888, when Sérusier came back from his summer vacation in Pont-Aven and showed his comrades a landscape painted on the back of a cigar box; they at once called it "The Talisman," for they sensed that it would change their art forever. Sérusier had executed it under the guidance of Paul Gauguin, who had asked him, "What color do you see this tree in?" Sérusier: "Yellow." Gauguin: "In that case, use your most beautiful yellow. And how do you see the earth?" Sérusier: "Red." Gauguin: "So use your most beautiful red." And so on, until the landscape was finished.

Under this impact, the friends decided to spread Gauguin's aesthetic gospel of imagination first, relying on pure color, decorative line, and simplified composition; and so they called themselves the Nabis (after the Hebrew word *nebiim*, meaning "prophets"). They invented a rite and held monthly meetings at which the group's theoreticians, Sérusier and Denis, proffered dogmatic statements such as "Remember that a painting, before being a battle horse, a nude, or some sort of anecdote, is essentially a flat surface covered with colors assembled in a certain order." At these meetings Bonnard was invariably present but, as in the *Homage to Cézanne,* at safe distance. Nothing could be farther from his nature than dogmas of any sort. "There is no rule," he once said. And indeed, the incredible freshness of his paintings, to the very end, lies in the fact that they seem improvised on the spur of the moment. Bonnard seems to have invented painting anew with every canvas. Never was he tempted, like so many colleagues, to set down in writing his canons of art; on one occasion when he felt the itch to take up the pen, it was to protest against the countless walls which prevent motoring tourists in France from fully enjoying the sight of the countryside. Nor could Bonnard, in spite of his sincere respect for his great elders, be an orthodox disciple. The group had chipped in to buy a Gauguin, which each member in turn could take home for a while; but Bonnard invariably forgot or passed up his turn.

Bonnard's playfulness and his amused, sympathetic attention toward the thousand and one manifestations of everyday life preserved him—as well as his close friend Vuillard—from the idealistic excesses of the other Nabis. Discreetly, quietly, he took Gauguin's flamboyant advice to throw off the academic yoke and interpreted it to suit his own modest needs: play hookey and indulge in that typically Parisian pastime, *flânerie* along the bustling boulevards. His best companion, on such occasions, was a short, worn-out pencil with which he sketched on a cheap pad; when without it, he would draw with anything that fell under his hand: a burnt match, a rusty nail, the tip of his finger dipped in a mixture of ashes and coffee dregs. His fondness for the woodcuts of Hiroshige, Utamaro, and Hokusai was due not only to their freedom of composition but to their intense interest in everyday life and to the decorative, casual "shorthand" they had developed to catch it.

Bonnard had only to come downstairs from his studio in the Rue Pigalle to plunge into the colorful whirl of Montmartre—the world of glittering, turn-of-the-century cafés and night clubs, of cab horses, waiters, corseted ladies, sidewalks bespattered with multicolored lights or lost in soft Paris grayness, that was made familiar by Toulouse-Lautrec. But whereas the latter's observation is ironic, incisive, even corrosive, Bonnard's is humorous and gentle. Lautrec captures his models with the lasso of his merciless line: Bonnard wins the confidence of the small girl with the enormous laundry basket under her arm, the nannies promenading their babies, the melancholy street lamps wrapped in mist, the woman sewing in the cozy circle of the lamp shade. His timidity reassures everything that is fleeting, fragile, and delicate in life. His paintings thus have the freshness of a secret whispered in your ear. What solemn historians call his "intimism" is simply his ability, unprecedented in art, not to domesticate dogs, cats, and children, but to let them stroll across his canvases (see for instance, *In Front of the Window,* opposite).

In a sense, Bonnard is one with them. Apart from a very few close human friends, he lavished his affection on a series of basset hounds. When his gardener at Le Cannet in the south of France one day prepared to use DDT against invading ants, Bonnard, over seventy, begged him to relent. Years before, at his home in Vernonnet along the Seine, he had come upon a wood dealer about to buy a tree from a farmer; Bonnard outbid him to save it from being cut down. Another time, a friend of his had fiercely condemned the horrid taste of bourgeois interiors, and in particular of their wallpaper; but Bonnard had asked for mercy for the wallpaper, for the sake of the little flowers on it

Wide-eyed, like a child, he takes in the message of the real world as though it were a fairy tale. A letter to his brother from the family estate at Grand-Lemps, in the Alps, conveys some of this simple magic: "Enormous heat. Everybody bathes, the little ones in the basin in front of the house and the grownups in the pond. There are heaps of fruit. *Maman* gathers them every afternoon in her basket. It is also nice to see our cousin in the big peach tree, amidst the branches and the blue sky. So, do come. . . ." Do come, his paintings also say to us; in them the world appears innocent, as if newborn, in constant flux, and eminently unpredictable. "Bonnard loves the accidental," Degas once remarked. In color, draftsmanship, and composition his paintings are no less unforeseeable, yet irrefutable. "Entering the house," Bonnard's letter to his brother goes on, "we found the little ones having lunch. Upon seeing me, Jean, waving his spoon, announces to me the big news: 'You know,

uncle, the cat has eaten the cream cheese!' He hadn't seen me in three months!" Bonnard's paintings are always surprising us by telling us about cats and cream cheese when we stodgily expect to be informed about some serious matter.

Everybody possesses the gift of childhood, but almost no one keeps it after he has ceased to be a child. It is a delicate plant, which Bonnard was able to preserve because of the particularly favorable climate of his time. It was a quiet, happy one, the last period of real peace France has known. Society seemed stable, tranquil. True, Bonnard and his Nabi friends were the avant-garde of their day, but the feats of their band in no way resembled the embattled, heroic, sometimes tragic adventure of their impressionist predecessors of the sixties and seventies. True, Bonnard met with difficulties, such as lack of recognition. Pissarro called his first exhibition at Durand-Ruel "a complete failure," and the owners of the gallery thought so little of his work that they never came to choose the picture that the artist had promised them in return for the loan of their exhibition room. But in those same years his father sent him the considerable allowance of 150 francs per month. The Nabis were professed anarchists, but Vuillard lived with his mother in reasonable comfort, and Bonnard's first studio was in his grandmother's flat. Bonnard proclaimed himself an anticlerical, but when a new-style priest, who had come to visit him in his old age at Le Cannet after the Liberation, saltily expressed his admiration for the pretty girls he had glimpsed on the Cannes beach, Bonnard commented drily, "In my time, priests commanded greater respect." Epoch, milieu, family, and friends combined to shield Bonnard from brutal upheavals and violent decisions, thereby providing his art with the peaceful atmosphere that it needed to blossom, as a child frolics in a sheltered park under the kindly supervision of his governess.

But there comes a closing hour for parks. An art so dependent on the protection of its time is in danger of going down with it. Indeed, that is what happened to Vuillard, who for years had worked in close relationship with Bonnard (somewhat as Braque and Picasso were to do in the days of Cubism). The turn of the century, which marked the end of the old order, also caused Vuillard's magic to wither. And here the case of Bonnard becomes still more remarkable. For while his erstwhile companion subsides into academism, as a retired person shuts himself up, all curtains drawn, in the cushioned silence of an apartment filled with souvenirs, Bonnard now throws open every window and lets light and color stream into his painting (as in *Dining Room on the Garden*). One would expect him to be blinded; but no, the sun becomes his ally, turning the earth into a golden honeycomb, filling the baskets with ripe fruit, the vases with luxuriant bouquets, and the bathtubs with *jeunes filles en fleurs*.

One of these *jeunes filles* may well have been the main reason for his new development. "A woman's charm," Bonnard later noted, "can reveal many things to an artist about

TEXT CONTINUED ON PAGE 25

On the following pages: a portfolio in gravure of paintings by Pierre Bonnard

IN FRONT OF THE WINDOW, 1923

MADAME NATANSON AND MARTHE BONNARD, 1928

DINING ROOM ON THE GARDEN, c. 1933

OVERLEAF: NUDE IN THE BATHTUB, c. 1935

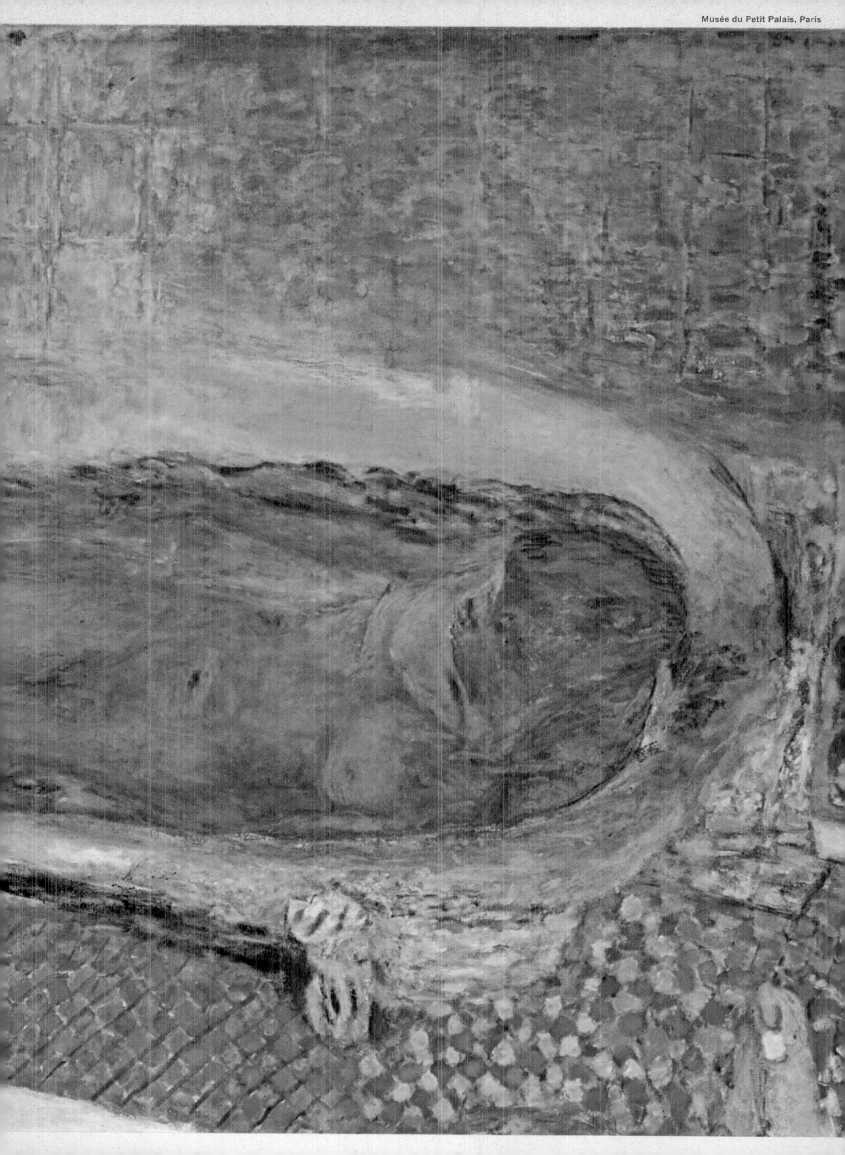

LUNCHEON, c. 1922

WALK BY THE SEA, 1924-25

TEXT CONTINUED FROM PAGE 16

his art." He saw her, a girl of twenty, in a Montmartre street one day in 1895, and at once, with the sudden boldness of shy people, spoke to her. She was to be his companion till her death in 1942. She told him her name was Marthe de Meligny, hinting at aristocratic origins, although she was more prosaically known as Maria Boursin and was simply a midinette. He believed her story—or pretended to—and did not find out her real name until 1925, when he married her, a gesture which meant so little to him that he had not even bothered to notify his family and asked his concierges to act as witnesses. Marthe, on the other hand, meant a great deal to him. She was to be the model for a long series of exquisite nudes, the quintessence of youthful loveliness (see *Nude in the Bathtub* and *Nude in Front of a Mirror* in the portfolio). What is remarkable about them is their combination of sensuousness and chastity. Degas's, Toulouse-Lautrec's, and even Renoir's nudes somehow betray the intrusion of a man's eye; those of Bonnard comb their hair, dry their backs, or put on their stockings with the easy abandon of people unobserved.

Marthe's tastes were simple. She loved sparkling bathrooms, fruits and flowers everywhere, and stunningly bright garments: perhaps it was she who introduced Bonnard to the realm of vivid colors. What is certain is that she was partly responsible for his rediscovery of nature. She was of fragile health; hence, after the turn of the century the couple tended more and more to desert Paris for the country. In 1912 Bonnard bought a ramshackle house at Vernonnet. Later still, in their quest for the sun, they moved to Le Cannet, a village above Cannes. And now, for the first time, Bonnard turned seriously to landscape painting, which was finally to occupy him almost to the exclusion of all other themes. "I feel weak in the face of nature," he said.

Marthe liked the country for another reason. She was pathologically shy and jealous: away from the city, she could have Pierre to herself. Here, he would not run off to see his friends on the pretext of taking the dog for a walk. Thus she gradually isolated him from society. Together, they would leave their house at Vernonnet for long motor trips through Belgium, Holland, or Spain, or settle in a seaside resort, Deauville or Arcachon, where Pierre, in order to paint, would tack his canvases against the walls of small, preposterously ugly hotel rooms. No doubt he sometimes found the weight of her tyranny heavy to bear. Yet he loved her as he loved no one else. He slept in an old iron bed in a monastic cell, but he himself made the furniture for her room. *His* paintings lay rolled on the floor, *hers* (she painted occasionally under the name of Marthe Solange) were framed and hung on the walls. When she died, Bonnard informed no one of the event, but he locked her room as it was and never allowed a visitor to enter it.

In fact, she had provided him with what he needed most: independence and uninvolvement. "When one paints, one can do only that," he once remarked. Unlike more strongly armored—if not stronger—personalities, Bonnard could not have withstood the pressure of modern life. He was acquainted with it, enjoyed it, but as an observer, a *flâneur*. He was passionately fond of walks and excursions and was one of the first Frenchmen to drive an automobile. He was spry and sporting, a good swimmer to the end of his life; and when he returned to Paris for the first Bastille Day celebrations after the Liberation, he could not, though nearly eighty, resist inviting a young girl to dance with him at a street-corner *bal public*. He would have loved the world, had the world consented to leave him alone. His pleasure at receiving a letter was immediately followed by a sigh: "Now I am going to have to answer!"

It is this fear of involvement, this determination to travel light, that explains the extreme sobriety and simplicity of his ways. Although his paintings had been bringing considerable prices since the 1920's, he lived and worked in conditions of near poverty, and often of acute discomfort. During the Second World War, when a friend, after having seen him writhe unhappily in his hard, bamboo rest-chair, brought him a mattress to make it softer, he firmly refused it: "Not that. I am not going to get accustomed to comfort at my age. Comfort means the end of liberty."

For the same reason, he refused the chains of riches. He kept his money in an old shoe box, and it was not until he was well over seventy that he opened a bank account. When he sold a painting, it was at preinflationary prices. "All those zeros make me sick!" he would say. Glory was as cumbersome as wealth—hence his boundless modesty. Someone reported to him that Picasso had made deprecating remarks about his work; his reply was to pin a Picasso on his wall—a reproduction, since the only original work of an artist in his possession was a small Renoir nude inscribed to him. He had turned down the Légion d'Honneur in 1912 (probably to protest the fact that Cézanne had been denied it); when, during the last war, he was again entreated to accept the honor, he answered, "When I was forty-five, I caused my mother the greatest sorrow in her life by refusing: Why should I accept now that I am seventy-six and alone?"

Emaciated at eighty, he still in his way looked as boyish as when he posed for Denis's *Homage* in 1901. This phenomenal preservation is even truer for his work, so fresh and clear that it excludes even the thought of a wrinkle, of a shadow, and of the effort that went into its making. Yet its childlike spontaneity is actually the result of painstaking labor. Bonnard's genius is ingenuousness recaptured by ingenuity. He took a great deal of time to complete most of his paintings. And he never really considered them finished: one afternoon, in front of an old oil of his at the Luxembourg Museum in Paris, he waited for the guard to go into the adjoining room, then quickly took a small paint kit out of his pocket and started touching up the canvas. Painting was a long, arduous journey through darkness toward a dazzling bright point on the horizon: the intense freshness of "the first moving, instant vision" provoked by an object. But actually to copy that object increased the distance from that vision. There is always the danger, Bonnard felt, of the artist's becoming caught by the incidentals of direct, immediate sight and losing the initial vision along the way. Hence, although he was more capable than anyone of catching what he saw, Bonnard always painted from memory: not by sight but, literally, by heart.

Perhaps this explains why, whereas the work of most talented painters is beautiful, that of Bonnard might be more appropriately called happy. It is like stepping into an enchanted land where all is light, from which hard edges are banned, and where—in the words of Degas—"nothing weighs or rests heavily." Bonnard's paintings always look broad and open, like a pair of welcoming arms, a fragrant fenceless garden, or a hospitable table decked with good things.

But if we consider it attentively, we shall find that this happiness is a strange one. Is naïveté its secret? One would swear so when one hears Bonnard say, "My chair always has a missing leg!" Then we discover another, more sophisticated remark: "The mistakes are sometimes what gives life to a picture." Or take Bonnard's colors: they appear radiant, yet upon closer inspection you find they are quite impure, and if compared with, say, those of the Fauves, downright dirty (just as the artist himself always managed to appear elegant although he bought his clothes second-hand). His harmonies are superb, but when analyzed, we realize that they *should* result in dissonances. Again, you may attribute your delight in Bonnard's world of painting to the fact that

it is purely imaginary, remembering his remark that "One must lie." Yet the painter Helleu, who had never met him, upon glancing at a Bonnard lithograph of people returning from the Bois de Boulogne, exclaimed: "But that's my wife and my daughter!" Or again, you may decide that his charm is a kind of belated impressionism, based on the play of light on reality, until you realize that—quite absurdly—in his pictures the sun can be dark and darkness sunny.

These contradictions are precisely the source of Bonnard's special quality. "I float between intimism and decoration," he once confided—that is, between faithfulness to reality and free play of the imagination. Bonnard's painting floats; it is suspended, liberated from gravity—which occurs only when two equal attractions cancel each other. Bonnard is *between*: between two centuries, between reality and abstraction, between awareness and dream. The surrealists painted dreams as if they were real; Bonnard painted reality as if it were a dream. All things remain identical to themselves, but are lifted into a state of suspension—exactly as in that state of floating between waking and sleep, after a siesta on a hot August afternoon, when we were children. Where does the room end, the garden begin? The shimmering, vibrant summer is everywhere. People move about, like silent shadows on the drowsy pool of well-being. More surmised than seen, the cupboard, the maid, the dog, only gradually emerge from the warm haze. And then, of a sudden, all things separate and freeze into their proper place: we are awake, purposeful, limited. Day and dream now go their separate ways.

So bright, so youthful was the summer which sang in his

The sensuous, sun-drenched canvases of Bonnard's later years were all painted in the bleak austerity of his villa at Le Cannet (opposite), which they brightened only momentarily—for as soon as he was done with one he rolled it up and put it on the floor. His only "collection" was tacked to his studio wall (left). In this strange assortment were a Picasso reproduction, a small Renoir original, some scraps of tin foil, three banal views of the Riviera, and post-card prints of works of art he admired: a Vermeer, a Monet, a Seurat, a Gauguin, a Greek torso—and a Bonnard.

canvases, louder with every passing year, that the death of the old painter with the delicate throat, on January 23, 1947, passed practically unnoticed. On the day of his funeral, the sunny Côte d'Azur suffered one of its rare snowstorms.

Bonnard was to become the victim of a worse irony yet. To understand it, we must go back a few years. In January, 1942, his wife died. A few months after, on the bad advice of friends, he forged a will for Marthe, according to which the deceased had made him her heir. Of course, Marthe had never owned anything. But they had married under community property regulations: some unexpected claimant among relatives on her side might turn up. To avoid bother, Bonnard committed the fraud. Never was there a more naïve criminal: he did not even think of disguising his own hand when he signed her name, and he dated the document as of the posthumous day when he wrote it.

Bonnard died untroubled, and thereupon the descendants of his brother and sister claimed the fabulous legacy he had left in his possession: some six hundred paintings, a large number of gouaches and water colors, and thousands of drawings (recently a single oil by Bonnard was auctioned for $100,000). A few months later, however, there appeared on the scene two nieces of Marthe, the Bowers sisters, whom even the late artist may never have heard of. They were ferreted out by an efficient genealogist. At any rate, they now claimed the heritage on the ground that Bonnard had forfeited his rights through his falsification; and so, they contended, had the heirs on his side, by not denouncing the fraud. A lawsuit began in 1947 and the contents of his studio were impounded. The law, which Bonnard had cavalierly

run out on as a student, now got its revenge. The courts in their wisdom decreed that all paintings completed before Marthe's death were indeed joint property, but not those unfinished or not yet begun at that time. But how was one to determine when a Bonnard picture is finished, considering that he would sneak into museums in order to retouch old works? Several of his oils were repainted twenty years after their "completion."

To clear up the imbroglio, experts were appointed and interminable discussions begun about the "moral right" of the artist to hold on to his work. One court broke the other's decision. New suits were initiated. One of the clans optioned off its prospective shares of the inheritance to various art dealers who began suing each other. Some members of one party deserted it to strike up an alliance with the rival party. Some of these contestants, now middle-aged and embittered, were the innocent children whom Bonnard had portrayed some forty years earlier: What better proof could he have found of the horror of growing up?

By now, the case has become an inextricable legal jungle. A new judgment is to be passed soon by the Cour de Cassation; it may well mean that the case will have to be tried all over again, and that will take many more years. Meanwhile, a good fourth of the total work of the master who had lived by the maxim, "Our God is light," lies buried in the darkness of a safe, in the Chase Manhattan Bank in Paris.

Pierre Schneider, an American art critic who lives in Paris, wrote the article on Poussin in the March, 1961, HORIZON.

A MEMORANDUM

From: Adolf Hitler

To: Professor A. J. P. Taylor,
Magdalen College, Oxford

Subject: Now that you have set
history straight again ...

Valhalla

I have received from below a copy of your book *The Origins of the Second World War*, newly published and widely discussed in several nations of the West. Up here it is usually twilight, and I am not reading much. Thereby I avoid tiring my eyes with the slanders of history-scribblers about my late earthly Mission. But your book is *different*. So different, Herr Professor, that I am pleased to extend you congratulations upon it. It tells not all the truth, but enough of the truth to reverse the recent tendency below to propagate the Lie.

I am glad to recognize, also, that the author is a distin-

guished professor at a University for which I have held the highest sentiments; did I not repeatedly tell that rascal Goering not to bomb it? Your Work—and I trust it is only the first of many that will find the right direction—proves to me the reawakening good sense of scholars in the West.

Your text, written in admirably clear English, reviews the whole history of Europe between the two wars and specifically absolves me of guilt for the second. Thus you write, "The peace of Versailles lacked moral validity from the start." Right! Precisely what I said from my own start. You declare that all I set out to do was to recover for Germany the "natural" place in Europe of which she had been deprived by Versailles. I could not have said it better myself. You show, correctly, that the Austrian crisis of 1938, which unfortunately forced me to take over that country, was precipitated not by me but by the Austrians themselves, and that "it was sprung on him [Hitler] by surprise." Next you prove that the Czech crisis that followed it was actually "of British making," not of mine. Finally you demonstrate beyond a doubt that when Poland's turn came in the following year, my objective was simply friendly "alliance with

Poland, not her destruction." Right, three times right!!!

You sum up that "Hitler did not make plans—for world conquest or for anything else." Here I must take exception, Herr Professor. Surely, you must grant that I made at least *some* plans! I was a statesman, not an idiot! But I agree entirely when you observe that "the state of German armament in 1939 gives the decisive proof that Hitler was not contemplating general war, and probably not intending war at all." How well you comprehend my situation then: with my thin line of Panzers, my still-raw recruits, and my wavering generals, how could I have possibly thought of aggression? Then I *would* have been an idiot!

I am grateful for so full a vindication, particularly when it comes from one formerly in the enemy camp. Clearly I owe it to the English sense of fair play. Once before, after Versailles, many decent elements in both England and America showed similar insight, and absolved my predecessor, William II, from all but just a little guilt. In my case, since I had been accused of so much more, your problem must have been greater, yet how completely you have overcome it, and how soon. One can always rely on an Anglo-Saxon gentle-

man's broadmindedness and his willingness to make amends.

For amends there must be. If I did not aggress, Herr Professor, then who did? Surely someone did! I think you have already provided the way to the answer. You write, for instance, that "the second World war grew out of the victories in the first." Rarely has a master of the historian's art expressed so much in so few words! For they can only mean that the Allied victors in the first war were themselves responsible for the second. And later you make yourself even clearer when you applaud the Munich settlement which your Mr. Chamberlain made with me by calling it "a triumph for all that was best and most enlightened in British life." Indeed it was! From this it must follow that those elements that repudiated Munich—your war-leaders, in short —represented the very opposite: all that was worst and least enlightened in British life. If Chamberlain and I were right, who was wrong? Since you correctly declare that I did not start the war, those who started it were evidently . . .

But I hardly need say the final word. From your own pages the conclusion all but leaps to the eye of anyone who can read English.   WILLIAM HARLAN HALE

AVANT-GARDE OR BLIND ALLEY?

What makes avant-garde art really and truly "avant"? New stylistic movements, as they come along, claim to represent the only sure and certain road to the future. But, more often than not, the future shows them to have been cul-de-sacs, detours leading nowhere. Why is this so? And how can we tell the difference between true and false, now, without waiting for the future to become the past?

By JAMES MARSTON FITCH

The truncated column (opposite) was designed by Mazière de Monville as an artificial ruin, to conceal the tidy interior (below) of a new suburban house near Paris. It passed for le dernier cri *in 1772*, when romantic ardor for antiquity was at its peak, but today seems absurd.

Louis Kahn's new laboratory for the University of Pennsylvania (right) may enjoy a kinder fate. Described as "the single most consequential building constructed in the United States since the war," it has compelled architects and critics alike to concede the merits of Kahn's distinctly personal approach, in which elements like the towers for air intake and exhaust are intended not only to serve their function but also to proclaim it.

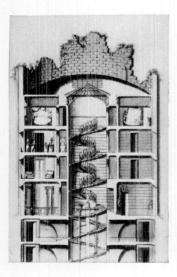

MALCOLM SMITH—ARCHITECTURAL GRAPHICS ASSOCIATES

One of the most striking features of the world of contemporary art is the unprecedented prestige that surrounds the new, the novel, the advanced. There has always been change in art, and it has always been welcomed by certain sectors of society. But until recently the new and novel had always to meet and win over to its side a conservative majority—a process that naturally took some time. Thus, at any given moment, the old form had always the support of the majority. By the time the new art won predominance, it had ceased to be new.

Things are quite otherwise today. A new stylistic movement needs only to be hailed as avant-garde by some critic or curator in order to be at once accorded the status of the significant, demanding our most serious attention and prompt applause. Any reservations we might express about the basic validity of the art form itself are dismissed by the avant-garde Establishment as reactionary. If we persist in airing our misgivings, this verdict is screwed shut (like the lid of an old-fashioned coffin) by a most persuasive historical analogy: all the great intellectual innovations of the past were always denounced by the reactionaries of their period. We are sharply reminded that the impressionists were barred from decent museums and that post-impressionists were called wild beasts; that Seurat was denounced as a charlatan, Picasso as a madman; that Bruno was burned at the stake and Galileo threatened with it for advancing innovations in celestial mechanics. Wrapped in this borrowed mantle of martyrdom, the newest artistic tyro gains an asylum from critical assessment as secure as any offered by the medieval church.

Of course it *is* true that social or artistic invention usually provokes a counteraction—the more profound the one, the more violent the other. Historically, the avant-garde *is* attacked as being either mad or subversive. This has certainly been the case with the great creators of modern architecture —Wright, Gropius, Mies van der Rohe, or Le Corbusier. It took them decades of resolute struggle to win over a decisive audience to their point of view.

But the current theory of the infallibility of the avant-garde is based not so much upon these noble precedents as upon a hidden corollary—namely, that *all* avant-gardes have proved to be of equal worth and durability; hence that *all* artistic dissenters merit the same respect as Picasso and Wright. History does not support this corollary so tidily. On the contrary, the record is full of movements hailed by their protagonists as the road of true advance, the unique and inevitable route to the future, which have nonetheless turned out to lead into cul-de-sacs, dead ends, wrong turnings going nowhere. And many an artistic innovator described as being a crackpot, poseur, or madman has turned out to have been precisely that. It is, in short, a clinical possibility for the artist to be mad, mistaken, or mediocre.

The whole argument turns upon what we mean when we use the phrase "avant-garde." It derives, of course, from French military practice, in the days when an army sent out scouts ahead of the main column to locate water and forage for horses and men; to spy out the disposition of the enemy; to sample the temper of the local population. From this practice derives the more poetic use of the word to describe one who explores and then sets forth for us the intellectual or artistic terrain of the future. But the favorable connotation of the term depends upon the *accuracy* of his reports. The avant-garde who returned to his army with incorrect information as to the whereabouts of forage or foe would

Reinforced concrete is the stuff of which avant-garde dreams are often made today. Because of its extreme plasticity, it lends itself both to the scientific rationalism of the Italian engineer Pier Nervi, who says that forms like his Rome Sports Palace, 1958 (below), are the direct expression of structural fact, and to the romanticism of the American architect Minoru Yamasaki, whose soaring pavilion (at right) is being built for the Seattle Fair.

promptly be punished as a numskull or shot as a traitor. If he wanted to keep his title, the future had to conform to his description of it. As a title of honor, avant-garde implies "mission successfully accomplished."

When we award this title to the great prophets and innovators of past times, we should remember that their own audiences felt compelled to wait for confirmation or disproof. Because of this inevitable time lag, the innovator himself was often dead of starvation or neglect before his audience could give him his just rewards. And even here we must be careful with the historic record, for sheer survival is, by itself, no absolute index of artistic worth. It would be nonsense to argue that *all* artistic movements that died a-borning died because they were "bad," just as it would be foolish to assume that all those that enjoyed a normal span of popularity thereby established their validity. Nevertheless, it is still demonstrably true that those artistic movements that responded to the broad social and cultural necessities of their time are the ones which proved most viable. The avant-garde establishment of today will be apt to deny that any such correlation is possible, but the proposition is quite readily demonstrated in architecture (as the portfolio in these ten pages is intended to show).

Today's avant-garde establishment has still another polemical weapon with which to beat back any objective evaluation of its activities. This is the accusation that the hostile critic, in denigrating a specific work of art, is secretly striking at the artist behind it. What is actually in jeopardy, so this argument goes, is not the artistic statement but actually the artist's right to make it. The avant-garde points out that artistic freedom in the modern world is closely tied to political freedom generally. Where one is infringed the other

is surely threatened. American artists have vivid proof of this from the recent McCarthy period, and they are understandably sensitive on the point. But here, too, there is an important corollary which is often overlooked. If we are to protect the artist's right to create and speak as his conscience dictates—if he is free to engage us, his audience, in a dialogue whose terms he sets—then, at this same level of civil liberties, his audience has the right of response, of query, even of rejection. The artist's right to speak to me should not rob me of my right of reply. Yet it is precisely this right that the avant-garde does not always recognize. Indeed, it often responds to any dissent quite as imperiously as ever did any old-fashioned academy or salon. And this suggests that, beneath a fancy dress of artistic nonconformism, there is concealed a new apparatus of vested interest—not an advance guard at all, but a rear guard.

The critic who accepts the self-proclaimed pretensions of the avant-gardists to infallibility, inevitability, and untouchability is trapped in a prison house of cliché. To escape, he need only apply a simple test: Does the future, as it unwinds, confirm their reports of it? The four great makers of modern architecture—Wright, Gropius, Mies, and Corbusier—have long since established their right to the title: the idioms they invented half a century ago are the basic grammar of the style today. But a second, and indeed a third, generation is now in the field, jousting for the right of succession. To whom should we listen? A review of two centuries' experience with other avant-gardists should help us to evaluate those who currently clamor for our support.

A professor at Columbia University's School of Architecture, Mr. Fitch is author of Architecture and the Esthetics of Plenty.

Paul Rudolph and the late Eero Saarinen are alike in saying that it is the duty of avant-garde architects to explore all possible modes of artistic expression. Concrete again adapts itself to such a philosophy, as is obvious in Saarinen's new TWA terminal in New York (above) or Rudolph's recent high school in Sarasota, Florida (at left).

Avant-garde or Blind Alley: continued overleaf

Decades ahead of the socialist Fourier, Claude-Nicolas Ledoux set out to create a style that would be true to the spirit of an emerging industrial society. This forge, with its extraordinary pyramidal smokestacks, was part of an unrealized project Ledoux designed for Chaux, France, in about 1775.

One of the earliest protests against the Renaissance order of aristocratic architecture came from among the aristocrats. Marie Antoinette's Hameau at Versailles was designed by Mique and Robert about 1785 to provide a rustic backdrop for the gamboling of royal shepherds and dairymaids.

Phase I: Utopia and Daydreams

The earlier avant-garde architecture of Europe and America often had its origins in Utopian literary or political movements. The buildings usually turned out to be more weatherproof than the novels or paintings, but they offered the same escape from mundane reality. Depending on the whim of the client, they could look forward (like the ideal communities of Claude-Nicolas Ledoux, opposite) or backward (like Mazière de Monville's contrived ruin, see page 30), or merely sidewise (like the rustic cottage Marie Antoinette caused to be constructed at Versailles, below).

But the style selected often seems capricious. To house his socialist "Phalansteries," Saint-Simon chose the aristocratic baroque; to counteract the boredom of royal elegance the Queen chose the archaic style of a peasant village; while to contain the King's state-owned armament industry Ledoux proposed a greatly simplified version of the classical. This latter mode then attracted the revolutionaries, like the painter Jacques-Louis David or the architect Etienne Boullée, whose noble forms for the new institutions of the Age of Reason in turn reduced the classical to a pure geometry of cube, sphere, and pyramid. Each of these styles was hailed in its day, by at least some group, as "advanced," "radical," *le dernier cri*—i.e., avant-garde. But history has modified such hopeful estimates. The more frivolous the needs of the patron, the more trivial was the scale of the architect's conception, the more odd his idiom—and the more certain his tumble into oblivion.

Etienne Boullée's revolt against the baroque found particularly dramatic expression in his purely geometric design for a cenotaph for Isaac Newton in 1784.

Samuel Sloane, Philadelphia builder and apostle of the occult benefits of living in octagonal houses, produced this Moorish delight for a Natchez planter about 1861.

With John Nash's Royal Pavilion, Brighton, 1815, the influence of the academic tradition was badly shaken.

Palm Stove, Decimus Burton's hothouse constructed in 1845, helped introduce glass and iron architecture to polite society. It survives today as a part of the Botanical Gardens at Kew, England.

Uncertain in his commitment to cast-iron Dobson hid his design for the Newcastle

Fonthill Abbey, designed by James Wyatt about 1798 for the dilettante novelist William Beckford, was a picturesque landmark in the rise of "Gothick" enthusiasm.

Phase II: Sense and Sentiment

Queen Victoria's century produced many schemes for man's improvement—public and private, secular and religious—and a corresponding range of avant-garde architecture. Buildings that served the matter-of-fact world of new social institutions tended, in general, to be rational expressions of volume and structure. But those for private persons tended to be idiosyncratic, filled with romantic allusions to the long ago and far away, while monumental and religious architecture, rejecting the materialistic science of the period, resurrected the medieval feudalism of the Gothic.

The division was never absolute, since Victorian architects crossed from one mode to another as their clients changed. Of the men represented above by some of their most straightforward work, Burton performed also in the classic style, Paxton in the "Elizabethan," and Dobson tried apologetically to hide his wonderful glass-and-metal train sheds behind a Georgian street front. Time has nonetheless proved that their Palm House, Newcastle Station, and Crystal Palace did in fact mark the road of true advance, while eclecticism led nowhere. At the time, however, men like the gifted Wyatt, with his preposterous lath-and-plaster "abbey" (at left), and the neurotic Pugin, with his plausible use of functionalism to justify a sentimental revival, as well as such oracles as John Ruskin and William Morris convinced Victorians that the true road to the future lay through the past. The result was one of the biggest detours in artistic history. It would require decades for Louis Sullivan in the United States to rediscover what Burton, Dobson, and Paxton had clearly stated: that sound architectural form can derive only from function correctly served.

onstruction pure and unadorned, Thomas
rain shed behind a conventional façade.

*Joseph Paxton's immense Crystal Palace for the International Exposition of 1851 at London was the
first major structure to dramatize the aesthetic possibilities which metal and glass had created.*

*Augustus Welby Pugin, the most responsible spokesman of Gothic revival, preached that a scholarly return to medieval design was essential to the
ritual needs of the Church. He assembled a number of his contributions to English church architecture in this imaginary landscape about 1840.*

Tony Garnier's proposed Cité Industrielle, *1904, though it offered no coherent new style, profited from the use of reinforced concrete to strip architecture of excess ornamentation.*

Le Corbusier's design for rebuilding Paris, in 1920, *in isolation but as an ordered environment to*

PHOTO MAS, BARCELONA

MUSEUM OF MODERN ART, N. Y.

Antonio Gaudi's attempt to abstract his forms from nature underlay such individualistic conceptions as his Casa Batlló, Barcelona, 1907.

Victor Horta, more literal in his translations from nature, designed a milestone of interior architecture, the Van Eetvelde salon, in 1895.

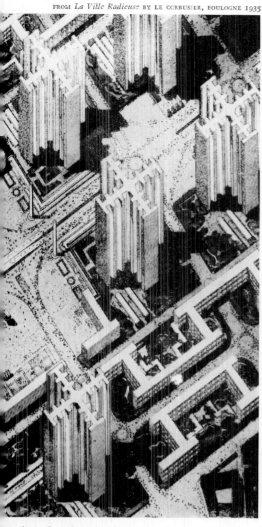

...envisaged urban architecture not as structures
...which all aspects of life must be accommodated.

In his futurist sketches for a Città Nuova, 1914, the Italian town planner and architect Antonio Sant' Elia anticipated much of the style that the 1930's would come to call "modernistic."

Phase III: Cold Steel and Warm Nature

Eric Mendelsohn's Einstein Tower, Potsdam, 1921, seemed admirable as a sketch but less so in execution.

The avant-garde architects of our century have been mainly serious, social-minded men who were stimulated by industrialism and have responded to its needs. Their attitudes have been evangelical, their work polemical in nature. But in their manner of expression, two divergent tendencies have appeared. One reflects the attempt to extract from the impersonal and repetitive aspects of industry a style that is pure, abstract, and supra-personal, independent both of historical motifs and individual caprice. Gropius and his Bauhaus (see HORIZON, November, 1961) have given us the clearest theoretical formulation of this point of view, while Garnier, Le Corbusier, and Sant' Elia (above) have produced dazzling images of its application to the design of cities.

At the same time, following a different path, men like Gaudi and Horta (opposite) handled the new raw materials as though architecture were instead a plastic medium for expressing a poetic vision. They could, when required, design perfectly rational apartment houses or trade-union centers, but the most complete and eloquent work of such individualists has been done for private persons who share their taste and can subsidize its realization in three dimensions. Their buildings have been hand-crafted, expensive, and—above all—unique (to build Gaudi's fabulous masonry, or Horta's spidery dome, requires the architect's continual presence at the site). The techniques are too specialized for mass production, the idiom too personal to be transmitted. Their work, like that of William Morris before them, is thus doomed to become a historical curiosity.

Two other giants of the period, Frank Lloyd Wright and Mies van der Rohe, have oscillated between these two extremes. Wright had two basic modes of expression: one a cubist enclosure of space, the other a plastic treatment of inner volumes. Mies, on the other hand, defines space by elegant, linear diagrams of steel and glass. Their solutions, formulated decades ago, are basic to today's vocabulary—proof of how well Wright and Mies foresaw the future.

What Will the Robin Do Then, Poor Thing?

By WALTER KERR

It is ungrateful of me, but I am disturbed by something that should please me: the temper of mind of the children I meet. I meet children because I have children, and I try to see them as the most worried and prophetic minds of our time wish me to see them: as intellectually undisciplined and emotionally overindulged, as soft products of a school environment in which the learning processes are corrupted into play projects and of homes in which too much permissiveness permits them to become flaccid captives of television.

Television has been invented just in time to take up the slack that has developed since educators decided against the wisdom of giving homework. Left to his own devices throughout the late afternoon, and having been taught to pursue his natural instincts rather than to think, the child lounges about reading comic books or sprawls in a chair before the television set. If his intellectual tone is limp from lack of exercise anywhere, his body tone is no better. This creature is sponge from head to foot.

At least that is the picture we paint of him when we are having one of our nightmares. And when one or another community or national crisis arises—a sharp increase in delinquency, a rumor that Russian children are managing calculus in fifth grade—the portrait seems grimly confirmed.

Now I must say that the exceedingly permissive rearing of the young has always appalled me. The abandonment of the intellectual and moral disciplines in school seems to me a sorry mistake. But without surrendering either of these views, and while acknowledging that I may simply have been lucky or may simply have not looked far enough, I am in honor bound to report that I have never yet met the nightmare we are so fond of describing, and I doubt very much that you have. The children I know, for instance, are in no real sense captives of television.

They look at television, of course, and will snap on the set just as often as permission is granted. But a captive is someone who cannot wrench himself loose from whatever it is that confines him. The children I know are not only able to free themselves at will from what is presumed to be spellbinding, they are able to free themselves without the least sign of wrenching. The drift away from the set is the most casual thing in the world. The young television audiences with whom I am familiar are vaguely mobile. They snap on a program, watch it for a while, wander off, wander back, exchange places from time to time. I am sure that the casual housekeeping gesture *I* perform most often is that of snapping off the set because no one is looking at it just now.

This can become a kind of game. Snap off the set and the probabilities are that within a minute or two it will be snapped on again by a nomadic child who has returned to the room and is conscious of his rights during the hours of permission. Having found the set turned off, he is likely to stay a little longer this trip. There are occasions, too, when an entire group will remain closeted with the set for an hour or more. But the probabilities are strong that during that hour or more the dial will be abruptly, skiddingly turned a half-dozen times—sustaining the easy, fragmentary character of ordinary, in-and-out viewing. On the whole, I would say, the children of my acquaintance are fond of television as one is fond of an undemanding dog or a familiar cat, and that they "watch" it in something of the way they watch adults: now and again in passing, as though mostly to make sure they are there.

Certainly it is the child that dominates the experience, not the experience the child. One is almost tempted to read contempt into so cavalier a treatment of so much expensive entertainment—an adult who wandered in and out of a concert or even a movie thus freely would be thought to be showing contempt—but that is going too far. The child does not feel superior to what he is seeing; he simply feels surprisingly objective about it.

I do see children reading comic books, perhaps especially when they are watching television. I also see them reading books. The books they read most eagerly are not what our image of the generation as uninformed and irresponsible would suggest: they are not even the contemporary equivalents of the Victor Appleton or Joseph Altsheler thrillers you and I might have wasted time on. The books they read are *The Monitor and the Merrimac, All About Snakes, The First Book of the Early Settlers, Getting to Know Malaya,* and *Thomas Jefferson: Father of Democracy.*

It would seem that contemporary children are a good bit freer of the television opiate and a good bit more dedicated to sober inquiry than our sometimes panic-stricken outcries proclaim them to be. I find that their conversation reflects the essential seriousness of their preoccupations. I am not myself particularly good with children; when one of my own brings a friend to the house, I am often distressed by my inability to hit upon a genial opening that will let him know he is officially welcome. But I have grown better at this lately because I have learned what to talk about. If, instead of asking artificially cheerful questions about his vacation or his prowess at fishing, I adopt an entirely adult tone and draw him into a discussion of the now-vanished land mass by means of which the original Eurasian tribes crossed the Bering Strait to Alaska during the fourth glacial period, I can establish almost immediate *rapprochement*. The problem after that is to get away from him.

Whenever we do notice that our children aren't wholly committed to television, that they aren't willing to offer it their firm concentration for any length of time, we wonder if this isn't one more symptom of their rootlessness, their restiveness, their eternal distractibility. It isn't. Though the twentieth-century child can be rather easily distracted from certain of the experiences available to him, he is fiercely tenacious about others. His attention can be held. It can be held by facts, by what is demonstrably true rather than by what has been only dramatically imagined. Hitler's Germany, the depression of 1930, the battle of Antietam, the rate of bank interest, the action of sperm cells, are subjects of endless fascination. When a child is found truly intent upon the television screen, the odds are great that he will be watching a stop-motion film in which the stamen and pistil of a flower are seen in the process of growth.

If these things are as true as they seem to me to be— if our children are psychologically free to take or leave entertainment and are drawn to sources of factual knowledge— what is there left for a father and a citizen to worry about?

It is precisely this inversion of the expected that disturbs me. I am disturbed by what may seem a small thing and may seem a sentimental thing but is nevertheless a real thing: by the fact that the modern child's mind is not susceptible to the attractions of free narrative.

By free narrative I mean storytelling for its own sake; storytelling that stands independent of any historical, scientific, or otherwise factual relevance and that finds its exhilaration within its own shapely, suspenseful patterning; storytelling that draws upon what is instinctive in the child and not on what is provable in the world about him. I mean the sort of "fiction" that takes its power to compel from a profound, though playful, tapping of the child's intuitions.

As the child turns from a form to which he has been overexposed and begins to investigate one far less familiar—as he turns to books, let us say—there is no fresh, native, innocent leap to the excitements of fiction. He is no more compelled by *Kidnapped* or *Heidi* or *The Prince and the Pauper* than he was by the ubiquitous Lone Ranger. Given a choice between a road map and *Robinson Crusoe*, he will elect the road map; I have seen the choice made. Publishers and booksellers have seen the choice made.

I am not convinced that it is a satiety born of too much television that has killed a generation's taste for fable, for fantasy, or for fiction of a most human kind. I do not think that it has been killed in the child at all. I think he was

born without it, or at best with an extraordinarily limited appetite. In our time, something has happened to the tides.

The contemporary child is a stranger to me, and not because he is coddled or spongelike or irresponsible. He is no prisoner of television; he is close to patronizing about it. He is no woolgatherer; he is a fact-gatherer. His habits are his own, obviously not the result of indoctrination: instead of being the victim of pedagogical tyrants determined to teach him useful things, he seems to have reversed a too indulgent pedagogical system and set about informing himself. His mind is naturally bent in a given direction; he likes that bent, and he pursues it because he likes it. He does not long for greener gayer hills. He is happy that his view of the universe is less "distorted" than mine was, and is happy that he knows more about the moon and pterodactyls than I do. He is, in his particular commitments and in the intensity with which he pursues them, admirable.

Making whatever exceptions or qualifications one wishes to make, it is impossible to conceive of this child as essentially pleasure-mad. He is not even especially tempted to what you and I would once have called pleasure. He is soberly devoted, generally, to what you and I still call work.

What disturbs me most about our admirable children is that the lifeline, the thread of release, the promise of a pleasure that is not in itself labor, seems never to have existed for them. They are not only accomplished in their command of what is useful; they are content with it. They will not have my memory of a foolish and useless and all-consuming passion; they do not want it. They will, I must conclude, grow to manhood without a nagging acquaintance with a possible alternative to their pursuits; they have not been interested in making such acquaintance. They will have single, rather than divided, minds; and the unquestioning simplicity of their lives may release them from feelings of guilt. But, given the sudden descent of a dark night of the soul, they will have no place to go.

It is almost as though the twentieth century had been engaged in a long struggle to produce a new kind of man—a man whose sole concern should be his useful work—and, in our children, had successfully accomplished the mutation.

Though they do not know it yet, I know that my children will one day come to a paralyzing moment in which everything they have loved is robbed of its flesh, a moment in which the circle of light that has long surrounded an object flickers sickeningly and its dimensions collapse like a retractable tin cup. For one of them a column of figures will straggle down a page in mocking unintelligibility. For another, geology will turn to so much carefully sifted dust.

What will the robin do then, poor thing?

Walter Kerr is best known as the drama critic of the New York Herald Tribune *and as a playwright. This essay will form a part of his forthcoming book* The Decline of Pleasure, *a critical examination of American society. It will be published in April by Simon & Schuster.*

Burial and Rebirth of a City in Love with Life

Pompeii

When the ruins came to light, they caused

a revolution in taste—stripping away rococo gilt,

reshaping the female figure, and leaving a

deposit of pseudo-Greek temples from Moscow to

Mississippi—although what sometimes passed

for "classical" would have bewildered the ancients

By NEIL McKENDRICK

An innocent-looking Vesuvius still "shaded with green vines" (as the Roman poet Mar-
tial saw it before the fatal eruption in A.D. 79) rises steeply behind the grape-clad figure
of Bacchus in this first-century fresco from a house in Pompeii. The snake is a sym-
bol of good luck, a sort of Pompeian rabbit's foot—and, in the event, no more effective.

43

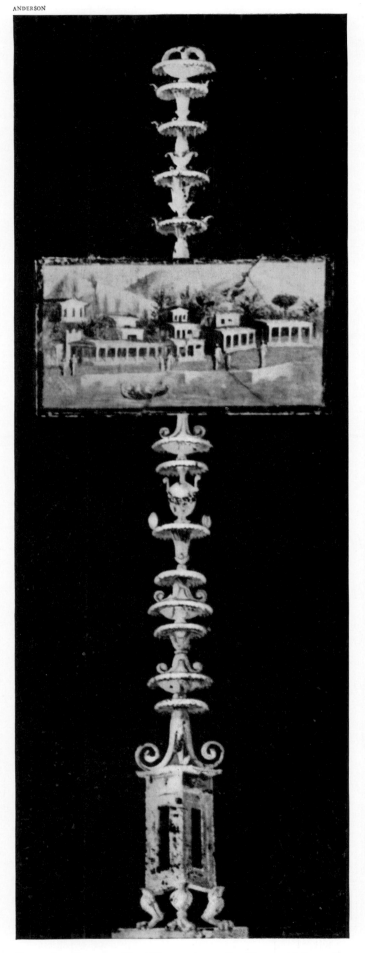

Pompeian frescoes like this one from the House of Lucretius Fronto greatly influenced late eighteenth-century decoration.

Before the two great natural disasters of the first century A.D.—the earthquake of 63 and the volcanic eruption of 79—Herculaneum and Pompeii had achieved a reputation for gracious and prosperous living. They were beautifully situated on the Bay of Naples; they were blessed with a delightful climate and a startlingly fertile soil; and they had enjoyed a peaceful, untroubled existence since Spartacus —the fugitive slave and famous gladiator—last threatened their security in 73 B.C. Not surprisingly, such a site had proved attractive to the rich, and the leisured classes of Rome were quick to flee from their teeming streets and noisy plebs for the easy life of Campania. The emperors themselves had set the pattern. Tiberius established his favorite residence on Capri; Caligula had settled on Ischia; and the whole shore line of the Gulf of Naples, from Cumae to Sorrento, was soon dotted with handsome villas and peopled with courtiers, generals, aristocrats, and the aspiring *nouveaux riches,* all living in contented and voluptuous idleness.

The reign of Augustus and the Pax Romana gave a further stimulus to trade, and the inhabitants of Herculaneum and Pompeii were among the first to enjoy the benefits. As they grew more prosperous, their houses grew larger and more beautifully appointed, their civic buildings took on a new grandeur, their bronzes and statues multiplied like weeds— indeed, their well-being was such that Martial was to immortalize it later in a nostalgic epigram ("It was a dwelling sweeter to Venus than Lacedaemon. . . . And all was consumed in the flames, all covered with the gray ash"). It was a world which could afford to indulge itself, and in such an era of luxury one would expect the decorative arts to flourish. They did. Almost every building contained fine paintings—from the villas of the aristocracy and the wealthy bourgeoisie to the shops of dealers and artisans, from temples to brothels. The frescoes with which the inhabitants adorned their walls, and the graffiti with which they defaced those of their friends, provide an accurate account of their daily occupations and the predominant interests of their leisured hours.

Trade was their major occupation, and trade was booming. The frank assurance of the inscription "Profit means joy" was based on long experience; and the cheerful slogan *"Salve lucrum,"* inscribed over so many Pompeian thresholds, seems rarely to have been disappointed. And with the increasing prosperity that stemmed from the Street of Abundance came a growing demand for luxury and good living. More and more monuments sprang up, magnificent statues were cast in bronze, and costly marble was increasingly used in building. A larger arena was built, a more sumptuous theatre was planned, and the baths in the forum were extravagantly equipped with hot and cold rooms and, to complete their comfort, an ingeniously planned central heating system. Urged on and supported by the convenient philosophy of Philodemus, who had skillfully adapted the teaching of Epicurus to justify a taste for luxurious living, the Campanians constantly extended their search for amusement and comfort. They had little use for Christianity, the latest fashion in religions, and preferred their own gods—greater in number and more accommodating in morals.

Indeed, the erotic adventures of the gods were easily the most popular subjects for frescoes: Jupiter was to be found almost everywhere, busily preoccupied with the seduction of Danaë, Io, or Leda, or, having been balked, with the rape of Europa. In a dozen frescoes Apollo hotly pursues Daphne, while Venus, even more heavily employed, shares her favors fifteen times with Mars and sixteen times with the beautiful Adonis. And when even the gods were exhausted, there remained ample erotic content to be depicted in the activities of the Campanians themselves. For their sensual preoccupations seemed to provide artistic inspiration at all levels: from the obscene frescoes in the *lupanare* (brothels), with their humorous Priapean drawings, to the magnificent set of frescoes of the prohibited Dionysian mysteries, which portray the flagellation of the naked postulant following the unveiling of the sacred phallus. And everywhere the walls carried the boasts of love achieved or the bitter complaints of unsatisfactory affairs—"What use to have a Venus if she is made of marble?" wrote one frustrated lover; while in the House of the Vettii is a room unashamedly devoted solely and entirely to the joys of Venus. Its walls are covered with stimulating pictures: each painting a different recipe in the art of love (not unexpectedly it has high tourist appeal).

Sex was not the only subject, however. Lurking among the ubiquitous gods, so constantly in search of their furtive pleasures, were magnificent examples of animal art—evidence of the Campanians' love of hunting and of gladiatorial games. There were young boars in mosaic, superb equestrian bronzes, the famous marble group of a stag struggling in the grip of hounds, and another of a vicious wild boar beset by hunting dogs. And everywhere stood magnificent busts and statues—dancing fauns, drunken satyrs, running athletes, and posturing gods—to delight the eye, indicate one's wealth, and exhibit one's taste.

In fact the general *ambiance* was one of sensuous and erotic pleasure, high artistic achievement, and lavish self-indulgence. But this atmosphere of peace, luxury, and sensuous delight was not destined to last. For suddenly at midday on the fifth of February, A.D. 63, from the heart of Vesuvius—that innocent-looking mountain "set in the green shade of grapes," so very different from the blackened industrial slag heap of today—came a terrible earthquake. The results were catastrophic—buildings collapsed, streets were blocked, six hundred sheep were engulfed by a great chasm which opened in the earth.

Many were killed and injured in the first shock, but most of the inhabitants fled to the countryside screaming in fear and execrating the gods for their treachery. Some never returned, and at first it was thought that the two towns would have to be abandoned, so great was the destruction. But

TEXT CONTINUED ON PAGE 49

TEXT CONTINUED FROM PAGE 45

gradually most of them drifted back, and the work of reconstruction began amid a welter of sacrifices and prayers designed to appease the angry gods.

Unfortunately, the forces that had shaken their world were no battling titans or displeased gods. They were all too natural, and indifferent to the powers of prayer. Moreover, the devastating earthquake of 63—it has been estimated to be of the ninth degree in Pompeii and Herculaneum—had not solved the problem. The pent-up steam and gases that were seeking an outlet in Vesuvius had gained only temporary relief. Sixteen years later, in A.D. 79, the tumescent forces broke out again like a monstrous angry boil and transformed the lovely towns into cemeteries.

Herculaneum, two miles directly below the summit of Vesuvius, fared the worst. The sudden torrential rain that accompanied the eruption mixed with the volcanic pumice stone and ash to form a terrifying avalanche of mud that swept toward Herculaneum and engulfed it. The inhabitants fled, leaving only the aged and the sick to suffer a miserable end in the all-engulfing mud. It flowed on inexorably. It penetrated everywhere. Soon Herculaneum was no longer a town: it was a vast tomb beneath forty feet of slowly hardening mud.

The fate of Pompeii, which lay farther from Vesuvius, was quite different but equally catastrophic. There was no stream of mud to force the inhabitants to flee: the danger here came from the sky in the hail of ash and lapilli. People sought shelter in their houses and cellars, where they were suffocated by the sulphurous fumes and then buried by the volcanic ash and pebbles. The loss of life was terrible. At

least sixteen thousand people died in Pompeii alone. Soon all were buried by the remorseless ash.

And along with the dead and dying, the wonderful statues, the beautiful buildings, the temples, villas, altars, and arenas were all engulfed. Herculaneum had disappeared in the mud and Pompeii was almost completely buried in ash and debris, which covered everything to a distance of ten miles in layers fifteen to twenty feet deep. In forty-eight hours a prosperous and flourishing area had been transformed into a grim heap of stones and ashes—the grave of thousands of men and women and a vault for priceless works of art. The two cities, their people, and their way of life were preserved under the ashes and mud like prawns in aspic. Even a chained-up dog, which writhed and howled its last in the House of Vesonius, was preserved in its contorted death agonies (below).

For more than sixteen hundred years the two cities remained buried. They had literally vanished from the face of the earth. Not that they were entirely forgotten—they lived on in the minds of men, as a reminder of death and disaster to the superstitious, as a temptation to those who dream of buried treasure, as a legend to entice the scholar and intrigue the archaeologist. They lived on in the singular, under the anonymous title of *"la Città,"* but only occasionally were they mentioned even as specifically as that.

Entombed in the first century A.D., they lay undiscovered until the Austrian occupation in 1710, when a peasant, Giovanni Battista Nocerino of Resina, began to deepen his well in an attempt to improve his water supply and came across great quantities of marble, alabaster, and other costly stone.

The death throes of Pompeii's citizens were preserved forever by the volcanic ash that engulfed them. Within this hardening shell their bodies decomposed, leaving behind not only the imprint of their flesh but of their clothing. By pouring liquid plaster into these molds, excavators made the pathetic casts shown here—a woman, a man, and a beggarman (opposite), a youth (above), and a writhing, chained watchdog (right).

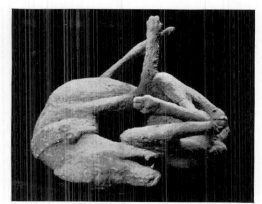

EDWIN SMITH—FROM *Pompeii & Herculaneum*, ELEK BOOKS LTD., LONDON

This aroused little interest at first. But then an Austrian colonel, Maurice of Lorraine, Prince of Elbeuf, bought the peasant's land and dug deeper in search of more of such excellent materials for the new villa that he was building nearby. He suddenly found himself the owner of a whole museum of antiquity. Precious marbles, decorated columns, bronze candelabras, and vases in profusion were discovered: most exciting of all, his workmen disinterred three magnificent marble statues of young women—for by sheer chance the well had hit right in the theatre of Herculaneum.

The first great step had been taken and the first great discoveries made. The three statues were shipped to the Belvedere palace of Prince Eugene of Savoy in Vienna, where they were exhibited in a special room and the art world flocked to see them. After such a triumph, surely the lost cities would now be revealed. But amazingly they were not. Elbeuf, discouraged by the absence of further immediate success, by the expense, and by the hostility of the natives at losing their subterranean treasures, discontinued his searches. Herculaneum sank once more into oblivion, an oblivion guarded and deepened by the activities of Vesuvius. Between 1717 and 1737 the volcanic activity was such that it has been likened to a continuous eruption, lasting twenty years and reaching a climax in 1737. With a constant flow of lava, flying debris, and sulphurous gases to contend with, no one gave much thought to Herculaneum.

Fortunately, however, those first discoveries were as restless as the mountain. Like artistic catalysts, they were constantly exciting interest in the art world and stimulating the connoisseurs to action wherever they went. And after being buried for sixteen hundred years, they were enjoying their freedom. In quick succession the three statues had passed from Elbeuf in Naples to Prince Eugene in Vienna and then on by inheritance to Anna Victoria, Princess of Saxony-Hildburghausen. Despite the protests of the whole Academy and the artistic world of Vienna, she sold them to Augustus III of Poland, who took them to Dresden. Such was his love of art that Augustus, when he acquired the Sistine Madonna of Raphael, had pushed back his throne with his own hands, shouting "Make way for the great Raphael!" He greeted the Vestal Virgins, as he mistakenly called them, more soberly, but he held them in equally high esteem and gave them a prominent place in his famous museum garden.

There they were seen and admired by two people who were to play vital roles in the further discovery of the two cities: firstly, the daughter of Augustus, Maria Amalia, who married Charles III, king of Naples, and carried her love of her father's statues back to their place of origin and, once there, prevailed on Charles to search for more; and secondly, Johann Joachim Winckelmann, the father of German archaeology, whose burning belief in the perfection of the ancients was fired by the statues at Dresden. "It deserves to be made known to the world," he wrote later, "that these three divine pieces blazed the way to the discovery of the underground treasures of the town of Herculaneum."

And he was right. For from 1738, when King Charles began his superbly successful excavations, Herculaneum was never lost again. Somewhat later, as if to clinch the rebirth of the two cities, a careless peasant fell down a well shaft and discovered Pompeii. These are the years that art historians often cite as the beginning of a new era, the start of that great classical revival which Gilbert Bagnani has christened the "Second Renascence." But such a claim is artificial. The interest in classical antiquity had never wholly died out, but it was to take far more than these early discoveries to spread the new fashion; it was not until much later in the century that it took root.

The discoveries, in fact, had little immediate impact on the taste of Europe. In the first half of the century, rococo was in fashion. The aim was still lightness, grace, asymmetry, and the inconsequential charm of disorder. Buildings were still a riot of movement; artists still aimed at color, gilt, and dazzling richness; porcelain had reached a state of airy perfection in the stream-ice fragility of Vincennes and Sèvres that was, perhaps, never to be challenged again. This was the world into which the art forms of the ancients were reborn: a world symbolized by Boucher's nudes and Fragonard's *Fête à Rambouillet,* in which the taste was for blooming roses, tinkling music, and beautiful women clothed in a froth of billowing silk and lace; a world in which "duchesses built dairies, installed a cow in a rococo setting, and to universal applause, milked it into a Sèvres vase."

But if rococo was at its height by the middle of the eighteenth century, it was also nearing its end. The challenge of the ancient world grew stronger through the 1750's, gained the upper hand in the sixties, and swept all before it in the seventies. It reigned supreme to the end of the century and beyond, until it in turn was dethroned by the romantic movement in the nineteenth century. As Archibald

TEXT CONTINUED ON PAGE 55

Opposite: In the great court of the Temple of Apollo at Pompeii, a bronze statue of the god, pulling back his bowstring, stands in silhouette against death-dealing Vesuvius.

Overleaf: Because they require digging through as much as sixty feet of hardened mud, the excavations at Herculaneum are less extensive than those at Pompeii, but they have uncovered the same rich décor in private villas and public buildings. The room at left, with its portrait bust and stucco walls painted to simulate marble, is in the House of the Bronze Hercules. The one at the right, with stucco bas-reliefs, swirling designs, marble-tiled floor, and wooden door still in place, is in the so-called Suburban Thermae.

Alison wrote in 1790 in his *Essays on the Nature and Principles of Taste*, "The Taste which now reigns is that of the Antique. Every thing we now use, is made in imitation of those models which have been lately discovered in Italy."

This classical taste was not the result of the discoveries at Herculaneum alone. They had needed powerful friends to storm the citadels of fashion, and they had been fortunate enough to find them. In the middle decades of the eighteenth century there was a host of able and willing allies to spread the city's fame and publicize its qualities. The Society of Dilettanti in England, the Grand Tour all over Europe, the new craze for archaeological publications, the prints of Giambattista Piranesi, the theories of Winckelmann, and the patronage of Sir William and Emma Hamilton at Naples were all vital agents in reawakening an interest in the antique. Without them, the discoveries might have languished —as the first successes of 1710 did—in the *Giornale dei Letterati d'Italia,* of interest only to scholars and specialists and completely unknown to the world at large. In Piranesi and Winckelmann, Herculaneum and Pompeii found the champions they needed, the true prophets of neoclassicism. While the Accademia Ercolenese hugged to itself the news of the finds, these two men trumpeted abroad both the discoveries and the general excellence of antiquity.

By 1750 Piranesi's great series of etchings was well under way. Urns, statues, shattered columns, overturned altars, ruined temples, baths, palaces, and amphitheatres poured from the press. Often they owed more to the artist's imagination than to historical accuracy—they were overgrown with vegetation, they were the haunt of beggars and thieves, and in their shadows pimps and prostitutes went furtively about their trade—but they brought the ancient world to life and made Piranesi famous throughout Europe. The glamour with which Poussin and Claude Lorrain had already enveloped classical architecture was heightened even further. Cochin's *Lettres sur les peintures d'Herculanum* and the successive volumes of the Comte de Caylus intensified the interest. Other printed editions soon followed. *Répertoires* and *Recueils* of antiquities were all the rage. Things did not have to be genuine to be included in these works: merely to look antique was enough.

But by far the greatest stimulus to the rising fashion came from Winckelmann. The son of a cobbler and at first destined for that trade himself, he was entranced by the ancient world. The Greeks to him were incapable of error, and he wrote of their statues with a passion that disturbs one by its very intensity. Greek art, Greek artists, and the Greek way of life were the perfect goals toward which one should strive. Nothing did more to stimulate the craze for the classics than Winckelmann's love affair with antiquity. His famous *Gedanken über die Nachahmung der griechischen Werke in Malerei und Bildhauerkunst (Thoughts on the Imitation of Greek Painting and Sculpture),* published in 1755, and his great masterpiece, the *History of Ancient Art* (1764), marked an epoch in the history of art.

The former began with the abrupt statement "Good taste . . . first arose under the Greek sky" and went on in eulogy of all things Greek. The author of these works even made the rather dubious point, to say the least, that the beauty of the Greek language, so rich in vowels, indicates that those who spoke it must have been exceedingly beautiful. But he said what the public wanted to hear, and these two books touched off a forest fire of neoclassical enthusiasm which blazed through Europe out to the edges of civilization.

Winckelmann said, in fact, little that was new: but he said it louder, more often, and with greater weight than anybody had said it before. He made mistakes, but they mattered little to the world of fashion. He was heard and he was believed. "Let no man," he commanded, "who has not formed his taste upon antiquity take it into his head to act the connoisseur of beauty: his ideas must be a parcel of whimsies." Ever ready to be directed, the world of fashion took note and then took action. From now on, to be classical was to be avant-garde.

Others had helped. In England the Society of Dilettanti had done much to stimulate an interest in antiquity. It was founded in the early 1730's, and its members were all young men of wealth and taste—most were peers or the sons of peers—who had returned from the Grand Tour with the intention of keeping alive their artistic knowledge and interests. Their social prominence alone helped to crystallize opinion in favor of classicism and gave further impetus to the growing fashion. But by far their most important work lay in their financial support of excavations and research into ancient civilizations. Stuart and Revett's famous *Antiquities of Athens* (first volume, 1762) and *Antiquities of Ionia* by Chandler, Revett, and Pars (first volume, 1769) were financed by the Dilettanti. In France these works were paralleled by Lercy's *Ruines des plus beaux monuments de la Grèce* of 1758; together they had a great effect. Excavation became the popular diversion of the day, and excavators equipped with little more than optimism, credulity, and perhaps a spade or two soon swarmed all over Europe. In this atmosphere the finds at Herculaneum and Pompeii took on a new glamour, and their influence was strengthened when in the middle years of the century Palmyra, Athens, Ionia, and Paestum were opened up.

The Vico Storto, or "Twisted Lane," is a typical Pompeian thoroughfare, narrower than some (it was probably one-way) but equipped with the steppingstones that enabled pedestrians to cross dry-shod from one curb to the other—an amenity overlooked by most twentieth-century cities.

Perhaps the most important vehicle of expression for the new discoveries was the Grand Tour.* The hordes of *milords inglesi* who flocked to the Continent to complete their education provided a wonderful audience for the excavations, and they quickly spread the word. As early as 1740, Horace Walpole, who was traveling in Italy with the poet Thomas Gray, saw Herculaneum and wrote in great excitement to Richard West: "We have seen something today that I am sure you've never read of, and perhaps never heard of. Have you ever heard of a subterranean town? . . . This underground city is perhaps one of the noblest curiosities that has ever been discovered. There is nothing of the kind known in the world; I mean a Roman city entire of that age, and that has not been corrupted with modern repairs. . . . 'Tis certainly an advantage to the learned world, that this has been laid up so long." Such letters had an immediate effect. Italy, the fountainhead of antiquity, became *the* place to visit, to see, to experience—indeed, some, like Lord Pembroke, held it to be the only proper place to learn to make love and recommended his former Italian flame to his son.

Once there, they may have taken Italian mistresses, but they fell in love with Italian antiquities. By education they were well prepared. They were already familiar with Greek and Roman literature, and a knowledge and love of the classical world had never died: Addison's *Cato* was but one of a long series of heroic dramas on Roman themes that entertained the theatregoers of eighteenth-century England; and in the seventeenth century Racine's *Andromaque, Iphigénie,* and *Phèdre* had similarly peopled the French stage with figures from Greek mythology. But the new discoveries gave fresh vigor to the classical ideal. To many the world of Greece and Rome seemed suddenly alive for the first time, and they flocked to Naples to see it: to stand amid the freshly revealed ruins, to marvel at their preservation, and to imagine the cities alive and lived-in.

Such experiences heightened the tourists' desire to possess some relic of this world. Ever since the Renaissance they

* See "The Grand Tour" by J. H. Plumb in HORIZON, November, 1959.

had collected classical bronzes, medallions, and marbles as souvenirs of their Tour. Now a whole museum of such objects awaited them, with the added glamour of the dramatic circumstances in which they were found and the voice of Winckelmann as a guarantee of their nobility and value. Flattered and delighted to discover that their hobbies had been raised to the status of scientific scholarship, the collectors and connoisseurs bought with renewed fervor, and they were willing to pay handsomely. A stream of objects —real, false, and indifferent—was soon flowing across the Continent to fill their studies and decorate their gardens in England. The world of fashion had gone Pompeii-mad.

The English visitors were extremely fortunate in their host, for Sir William Hamilton, Plenipotentiary at Naples for thirty-six years (1764–1800), was both warmly hospitable and immersed in the new discoveries. He might occasionally tire of the hordes of tourists and write wearily and ironically to Walpole, "I respect Magna Charta, but wish there had been in it some little restraint upon emigrants," but he never failed to entertain his visitors, or to instruct them in the finer points of the excavations. As enthusiastic as he was knowledgeable, he never tired of showing his visitors over Vesuvius and the new finds, on both of which he was a very considerable expert. As a close friend of Queen Maria Carolina of Naples, he had easy access to the excavations, and his guests were rarely disappointed, for it had become the custom at Herculaneum to "lay on" finds for distinguished visitors. Fine bronzes and particularly impressive statues were carefully reburied and brought to light with excited cries of surprise and congratulation just as the visitors arrived or immediately after they had moved their first spadeful of earth. The most spectacular finds were kept, if possible, for Queen Maria Carolina herself. Her delighted enthusiasm—and her splendid tips—more than repaid the thoughtful timing of such discoveries. For even the most unimportant visitor, the diggers could usually manage a coin or a marble fragment, if he was accompanied by Sir William.

However, Sir William had more to offer than hospitality,

TEXT CONTINUED ON PAGE 61

The Villa of the Mysteries

The frescoes reproduced on the four following pages are part of a remarkable frieze uncovered in 1930 in a villa on the outskirts of Pompeii. It depicts the initiation rites of a Dionysiac mystery cult, but in such a way as to make precise interpretation difficult for the outsider. Thus, when a priestess is shown presiding at the ritual table (opposite), her back is turned to us and we cannot see what lies in the basket. At the climax of the ceremony (overleaf), two hands reach out to unveil an image of the sacred phallus, which stands under a cloth in a winnowing basket, and a figure wearing huge wings raises her whip to flagellate the trembling postulant—who submits to the purifying blows (third panel) while a bacchante dances to the clash of cymbals. But even more dramatic than this symbolic union with divine fertility is the woman (page 60) who freezes in terror at the sight of the flagellation, while next to her a member of the Dionysian retinue—a Panisca, or "daughter of Pan"—unconcernedly suckles a kid.

56

TEXT CONTINUED FROM PAGE 56

expert knowledge, and an entree to the excavations. He had also "a living antique," his lovely young mistress, Emma who later became his wife and then the mistress of Lord Nelson. Sir William had acquired her from his nephew Charles Greville, who in the course of a correspondence which startles one by its cold-blooded common sense and un-inhibited frankness, assured him, "You will have comfort with the prettiest woman confessedly in London. The poets and painters would say more . . . a Modern, who will not render your criticisms of the Antique less pure." As Goethe wrote, "In her, he finds the charm of all antiques, the fair profiles on Sicilian coins, the Apollo Belvedere himself."

Apart from her beauty, she possessed a charm and gaiety of manner that captivated her most hostile critics and an acting skill that she employed in her "Grecian attitudes." Draped in a few yards of gauze, and standing in a black-lined box framed in gold, Emma entranced European society by portraying the various attitudes of the figures found at Herculaneum and thus won for them new fame all over the Continent. The cynics may say that she was merely adapting the skills she had learned while posing in indecent *tableaux vivants* in the stews of London, and they may well be right, but it did not affect her popularity. Her Grecian eurythmics, as they came to be called, were copied by hordes of aspiring hostesses in every European capital.

With such influential patrons, Pompeii and Herculaneum were bound to prosper. Sir William was the foremost connoisseur of his time, and he drew shoals of visitors; Emma, once Romney's model, was equally at home with artists and the artistic world; and with Winckelmann and Goethe to give the final seal of aesthetic approval, Naples soon hummed with artistic activity. No artist could afford to miss a year or so there. Before the reign of George III, artists had studied the antique and the Renaissance with equal zest. But when Academy students were sent to Italy in the 1750's, they were instructed to concentrate on the glorious antique. The moderns had become anathema to all: Winckelmann had written that "imitation of the Ancients is the shortest way to perfection in the fine arts," and clearly those painters who most nearly resembled them would be the best.

With each passing year the attraction of Pompeii and Herculaneum grew stronger. There were constant new surprises, and the continual hope, rarely disappointed, of more to come. Such progress kept the discoveries in the news. The changing pattern revealed by the excavations meant that the spectacle never staled, and each fresh find added to the tourist appeal. There was always the hope of witnessing some momentous discovery and always the likelihood of seeing things unknown to the world the previous year. And finds of such astonishing richness as Karl Weber's discovery of a great peristyle in 1750 could be counted on to send interest soaring to new heights. Classicism had become *le dernier cri*.

No one was quicker to exploit this new demand, and no one did more to further the classical fashion, than Josiah Wedgwood.* He changed his style and became the prophet of the new art form. It was to this realization of the possibilities of neoclassicism—while his rivals still busied themselves with what he called "a dazzling profusion of riches and ornament"—that Wedgwood owed much of his success. He had first use of a market "randy for antique." He did everything he could to promote and serve the new fashion. He based his vases on the urns and amphorae of the ancients; he decorated them with classical swags and garlands; he reproduced their cameo medallions and reclining figures. He invented new glazes to suit their designs and revived encaustic painting to decorate them. He named his new factory "Etruria" and inscribed on its first products the words *"Artes Etruriae Renascuntur"* ("The arts of Etruria are reborn"). He was, of course, like everyone else, mistaken in thinking that Pompeii and Herculaneum were Etruscan; but mistaken or not, his loyalty to the antique was unswerving.

In only one way was he unfaithful to his classical models: when English society found the uncompromisingly naked figures of the ancients "too warm" for its taste, and the ardor of the Greek gods too easily apparent, Wedgwood was quick to cloak their pagan immodesty—gowns for the girls and fig leaves for the gods was the usual arrangement. But as he once had to remind one of his artists, John Flaxman, "Fig leaves are not always enough," and in these cases the figures were completely redraped.

Although this often corrupted the original source—Priapus, for instance, was so draped and beflowered in Wedgwood's version as to conceal his purpose in life—it did little to harm his popularity. Such was his success that his rivals were forced to follow suit and copy his designs. Not only the humble Staffordshire potters, who were used to basing their policy on the dictates of his fertile genius, but the great continental factories of Sèvres, Meissen, Frankenthal, Doccia, Vienna, Paris, and Fürstenberg all had to follow his lead and reproduce Wedgwood designs. Where once rococo whimsy had run riot, now antique severity reigned.

Others were also responding to the demands of the new market. As the rage for the antique and the excitement over Herculaneum grew, the proliferating decoration, the exuberant colors, and the universal gilding of rococo were banished; the splendors of baroque became distasteful; the intricacies of *chinoiserie* lost their favor. The new fashion was eagerly taken up by architects and interior decorators, and a trail of painted interiors, based on the frescoes at Herculaneum and Pompeii, soon stretched across the length and breadth of the Continent: from Robert Adam's ceilings at Mellerstain and Syon in Britain to Marie Antoinette's apartment in the new Louis Seize style at Fontainebleau; from the Czernin Palace at Vienna to Catherine the Great's palace at Tsarkoe Selo in Russia. Such a mode had, of course, its critics. They likened the new style with its cameos, me-

* For a discussion of this, see "Josiah Wedgwood and His Friends" by the author of this article, in the May, 1959, HORIZON.

Robert Adam

Sir William Hamilton

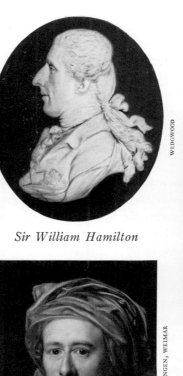

Johann Winckelmann

Queen Maria Amalia

There was no serious effort to uncover Pompeii and Herculaneum until 1738, when the king of Naples—spurred on by the enthusiasm of Queen Maria Amalia—began to excavate the latter. Twenty years later it was visited by the German classicist Johann Joachim Winckelmann, who came back proclaiming the "voluptuous tastes" of the buried cities. During his long tenure as the British envoy to Naples, Sir William Hamilton regularly conducted visitors to the excavations; and in England the Campanian decorative technique of stucco arabesques was popularized by the great architects Robert and James Adam. All this brought the Grand Tourists flocking to Pompeii, where some of them were depicted inspecting the Temple of Isis (opposite) in an etching by the son of Giambattista Piranesi.

dallions, and filigree ornament to "The Twelfth Night decoration of a pastry cook," or mocked it as "the knickknackery of the cabinetmaker," and scorned the "rampant foliage of antiquity." But the antique was proof against such envy. In some cases it was spurred on by it: as Mrs. Montagu smugly congratulated herself in 1767 on her new Adam decorations, they "are pretty enough to make me a thousand enemies. Envy turns livid at the first glimpse of them."

The classical vogue never, however, enjoyed a complete monopoly. Some were frankly unappreciative of the antique: Napoleon's soldiers, having captured Naples, whiled away the hours by practicing with their cannon on a magnificent equine marble, and, as one might expect from Napoleonic artillery, they were accurate and shot off its head. But even among the more discerning there were pockets of resistance. Rococo was a long time a-dying in some places, *chinoiserie* still had its adherents, and Gothic was even showing signs of a revival. Horace Walpole built Strawberry Hill in Gothic, and Beckford did the same at Fonthill; and the Pagoda at Kew was not the only example of the Chinese style. But for the most part these were charming backwaters, whose importance in relation to the taste of their times has often been exaggerated. The mainstream of European taste was flowing strongly toward the antique, and Horace Walpole's Strawberry Hill was, as he said himself, merely a temporary

infidelity from the true mistress of the age, the antique.

Others were more faithful: the Adam brothers, Chalgrin, and Schinkel scarcely deviated from the antique pattern in their architecture; and London, Paris, and Berlin were soon dotted with handsome buildings of wholly classical design.

No one had a greater influence in this sphere than Robert Adam: indeed, he is often taken as the most complete expression of the neoclassical revival. A cherished friend of Piranesi and possibly an acquaintance of Winckelmann, he had spent three years in Italy and Dalmatia (where he visited the palace of Diocletian at Spalato with the French architect Clérisseau) in order to perfect his knowledge of antique architecture. He returned to England boldly declaring his intention of introducing a mode of decoration different from "anything hitherto practised in Europe," with style and ornaments "imitated from the vases and urns of the Etruscans." Soon he was the architect of the hour. "The whole town is run mad after Adam," wrote one disgruntled rival. In the sixties the great houses of Mersham-le-Hatch, Syon, Osterley, Kedleston, Lansdowne House, Luton Hoo, Harewood, Kenwood, and Saltram were all begun, and Robert Adam and his brother James could reasonably congratulate themselves, as in fact they did, on having captured "with some degree of success . . . the beautiful spirit of antiquity" and made it prevail in a new fashion in all their

works. By the 1770's their conquest was complete: the rich had Adam, and the middle classes had Adamesque. There was complete coherence of taste.

As in architecture, so in other art forms: Pompeii and Herculaneum set the tone. Their influence is visible in every material and in almost every facet of life. Even men's dress followed the prevailing trend, with Beau Brummell giving the lead. He applied those principles of restraint, natural-ness, and simplicity, the Georgian version of Winckelmann's famous slogan of "noble simplicity and calm grandeur," to his personal appearance. The result was a style more austere and more dignified than any before or since. It soon domi-nated the world of fashion, and its influence is with us still. The chaotic history of male costume, alternating between the too fine and the too coarse, came to a close on "that bright morning," to quote Max Beerbohm, "when Mr. Brummell, at his mirror, conceived the notion of trousers and simple coats." Women's dress had, of course, fallen into line with the new fashion much earlier. By 1787 the new "Grecian mode" was already making inroads on the hoop petticoat: by some it was held to be indecorous, for the soft gowns clung to the figure "like wet drapery" and revealed it for all to see; by others it was held to be dangerous, for no modest female, they said, was safe without her hoop—it was the rampart that protected her virtue. Fashion, how-ever, has always triumphed over virtue and decorum. The lady of fashion threw away her hoops, kicked off her petti-coats, put on knickers, and dropped her neckline danger-ously low. And her figure, if we can take art as our mirror, followed the pattern of her dress and changed to more clas-sical proportions. The round rococo nudes that had bounced across Boucher's canvases or frolicked in a Fragonard land-scape were very different from the stately ladies drawn by David and Ingres. Like everything else, the female figure had to conform to the ideal.

Not only was their shape changed, but their attitude and posture. Where Boucher's Miss O'Murphy had sprawled in-vitingly bottoms-up on her silk-cushioned sofa, and where Watteau and Rubens had sought inspiration in the ample buttocks of their models, the neoclassical artists' approach was almost exclusively frontal. "The bottom," Sir Kenneth Clark has said, "is a baroque form," and as such it had to go. The new line was harder, more severe, more classically correct. Where the baroque and the rococo "gave promise of pneumatic bliss," the neoclassical promised pleasure only to necrophiliacs. The flesh had hardened into marble.

The pendulum of European art had swung once more: it was Renoir who said, "The female nude rises from the sea or from her bed; she is called Venus or Nini." In the early eighteenth century Nini reigned supreme. Gay, charming,

TEXT CONTINUED ON PAGE 68

63

The French Turn Greco-Roman

When Queen Marie Antoinette took up classically inspired styles, fashionable France quickly followed suit—whether she dressed her hair in antique curls (above) for her Trianon fêtes or decorated her boudoir at Fontainebleau (opposite) in a Gallicized version of Pompeian arabesques. This combination of fragile sylvan motifs and mythological subjects came to be known as the Louis XVI style, which corresponded to the creations of the Adam brothers in England. The swirling tendrils on the panels and doors of the boudoir resemble the fragment from the ancient House of the Vettii (left) in which Psyche gathers flowers beneath slender, garlanded columns. Inset in the boudoir's mahogany commode are two Sèvres plaques of bacchantes—one beating a tambourine, and the other holding a branch of peace—which were copied from dancing figures (below) found in the so-called Villa of Cicero at Pompeii. A Sèvres bust of the Queen rests on the commode, and above the door is an allegory of sacred and profane music. Gossipy Mme de Staël wrote to Gustavus III of Sweden that the boudoir was beautiful beyond anything that could be imagined; and there was even an unlikely rumor that Louis XVI himself was inspired to carve the decorative metalwork for the windows (not seen here).

The Old Becomes the New

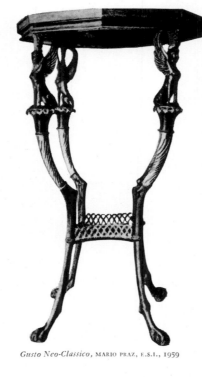

Above: The most "classical" of painters was the Frenchman J. A. D. Ingres, who magisterially proclaimed that to study anything but the antique was madness. After being exposed to old Campanian art during a visit to Naples in 1814, he copied the pose of the regal Arcadia (left)—whom he had seen in a fresco in the Basilica of Herculaneum—in his portrait of Mme Moitessier (right).

Left: This ornate bronze tripod from Pompeii (far left) has had a continuing influence on furniture design from the eighteenth century to the present day. In a more graceful four-legged adaptation (near left) it even turned up in Russia, where it complemented the classical décor of Pavlovsk, a country house built for the Grand Duke Paul.

Below: One of the most successful imitators of the antique was the potter Josiah Wedgwood, whose wares blossomed with "Herculaneum figures." Among them were two statues of the Muses found in Campania: Thalia with her crook and mask (left) and Melpomene with her club (right). Wedgwood copied them on an elegant blue jasper vase (bottom).

Above: A relief of the three Graces, based on a Pompeian fresco (top), adorns a marble mantelpiece in Syon House near London. The Duke of Northumberland had instructed Robert Adam to design a house in the antique style. "The idea was to me a favorite one, the subject great," wrote Adam, adding enthusiastically, "and the expense unlimited."

*Taking frescoes of Campanian bac-
chantes (above) as her model, Lady
Hamilton, wife of the English envoy
to Naples—whose interest in Pompeian diggings was equaled only by
her own in Lord Nelson—was painted in one of her famous "Grecian attitudes" by George Romney (opposite).*

TEXT CONTINUED FROM PAGE 63

and lively, she bounced around in pink and plump profusion
and offered herself to one's inspection without standing on
ceremony, only to be banished into the background in the
1770's, like a skittish parlormaid on the return of her stately
mistress, Venus. The eternal classical beauty, exhumed from
the ashes of Pompeii, quickly recovered her authority and
enthroned herself in a court of uniformly sculptural beauties
with the bashful and frigid Psyche as her chief lady-in-
waiting. The change is symbolized by the tastes of Mme
Pompadour and of Marie Antoinette: under the Pompadour
rococo was all the rage, and she herself was painted by
Boucher, naked and frolicking in a rococo setting; under
Marie Antoinette, everything eventually had to be *à la
grècque,* and she herself, decked in Grecian robes and crowned
with a laurel wreath, sat in the Trianon and played on an
antique harp.

In only one major aspect of artistic life was the antique
influence weak: it had little immediate impact on literature.
It is not difficult to see why. The discoveries at Herculaneum
and Pompeii, thrilling though they were as historic incidents,
disclosed no new material to inspire a man of letters. Ar-
chaeologists, scholars, connoisseurs, and artists were agog,
but there were no Greek or Roman manuscripts brought to
light, such as were discovered in the Renaissance, to renew
the classical tradition in literature. There was, indeed, the
odd exception: Keats's *Ode on a Grecian Urn* is a charming
example of the new enthusiasm for the antique inspiring one
of the most romantic of poets. But for the most part writers
turned to romanticism to explore fresh fields of emotional
experience or turned back to the Middle Ages and wallowed
in its Gothic horrors.

But while writers looked forward in hope, the rest of the
world of art looked back in awe. The resurgence of the classical had free play, even if some of its forms would have
surprised a Greek or a Roman. Although the antique was the
touchstone of perfection, the eighteenth century was somewhat indiscriminate in its sources. The product had to be
classical, but whether the source was from Rome of the first
century A.D., Greece of the fourth century B.C., Italy of the
quattrocento, or England of the eighteenth century, as long
as it *looked* antique it would sell. For anything that was
ancient was excellent. And so across the ceilings of Europe,
across its pottery, its tapestries, and its canvases, danced a
frieze of assorted gods and goddesses banging cymbals, playing harps, carrying urns, and decked out in flowing veils.
The coiffures were sometimes modified, the nudes were sometimes fig-leafed, and their actions often invented—but their
classical inspiration was unmistakable. And if they differed
a little from the purity of the original, it is hardly surprising, for as George Boas assures us, "Each age creates its own
Greeks," and the eighteenth century was more than satisfied
with its version.

Neil McKendrick, whose earlier article for HORIZON *is mentioned in the footnote on page 61, is a Fellow and College Lec-
turer in History at Gonville and Caius College, Cambridge.*

THE COMING GENERATION OF GENIUS

A Chicago scientist speculates on the quality of intelligence and tells why he believes America may have created the conditions for an "explosion" of 180-IQ boys. And girls?

By JOHN RADER PLATT

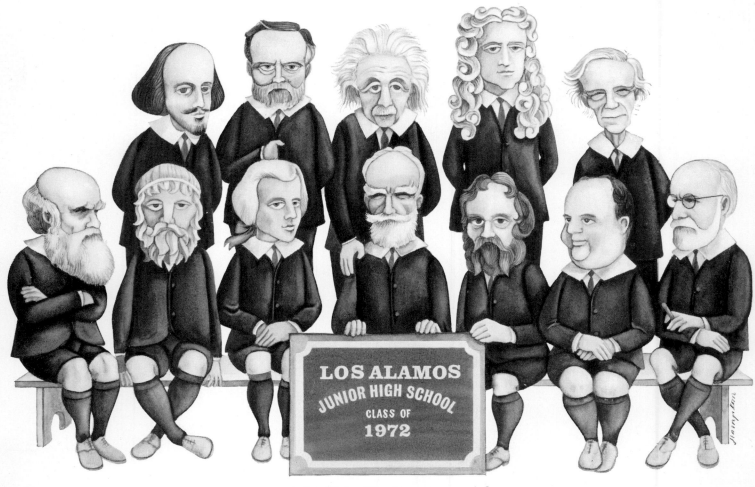

Artist Blake Hampton was carried away by the author's speculation that American schools may soon turn out students like another Darwin, Archimedes, Mozart, G. B. Shaw, Galileo, John von Neumann, Freud (front), and Shakespeare, Pasteur, Einstein, Newton, Bertrand Russell (standing).

The differences in the looks and the behavior of human beings have always been a marvel to me. I remember, when growing up in Florida, there was one man in our community—a good man—who looked like a gorilla. He had long hairy arms and a barrel chest, and when he laughed, which was often, it was a coarse furniture-rattling laugh such as I imagined a gorilla might make if he had been given the power of laughter.

Later, when I went off to college, my sensitivity to the varieties of appearance and character had been sharpened. I began to see many men whom it amused me to classify privately as resembling one bright-eyed animal or another. In the course of some years of university teaching, I have known and liked one tarsier well, and a Great Dane, and a couple of bullfrogs; and there was one favorite vegetable professor who looked like an unmade bed and talked like a pillow. Of course I suspect that, like the fellow in the song about the Eddystone Light, after you have counted the porpoise and the porgy, the other is me; and I probably look like some queer animal, too (I won't guess what), pedaling off down the street with what hair I have left stuck out akimbo in the wind.

But the remarkable thing about it is that among men who really know something, the looks quickly cease to matter. I remember very clearly the dinner party where I first met L. L. Thurstone, the engineer who became a psychologist and developed the powerful statistical method called factor analysis. At first I thought he was one of the homeliest men I had ever seen. I have a memory of piercing eyes, and ears like sails, and a nose that seemed to have grown at random. But within ten seconds after he began to talk, I could no longer see the face at all, for I was looking at a mind. The excitement of hearing his reasoning and his experience led the whole party out into an arena of intellect where such trivia as looks and clothes, the room, the dinner, all faded into the background. I think we rose not knowing what we had eaten and had brandy afterward not knowing what we were drinking, we were so wrapped up in the flow of conversation.

Around a good university the minds are the realest things there are. And after a little while you realize that it is not only in our external looks that we resemble various strange unkempt animals but in the shapes of our intellects, too. Each has its peculiar distortion. The mental ears stick out; the brain has its own hairy and primitive arms. But I think I also see the shapes of many wonderful new patterns of mind that cannot any longer be compared even fancifully to animals because they are types that have scarcely existed in the world before.

It is interesting to look at these gross differences in the kinds of intelligence and at the new races of mind that may be slowly evolving among us, like the intellectual fingers of mankind reaching and spreading out to unknown ends.

There are three kinds of mental difference that impress me most: the difference between men and women, between genius and stupidity, and between different creative talents. The differences between the minds of men and women are numerous, and we often joke about them. If a man's car hits a laundry truck and he phones his wife about it, the first thing she asks is the name of the laundry. Are such differences in outlook innate, a matter of sexual difference in brain physiology and organiza-

tion? Or are they cultural, imposed perhaps in childhood by the different expectations and behavior of the adults in our society toward the growing boy and girl?

For example, are men dominant and women submissive? Not necessarily innately. Matriarchal cultures ruled by women have flourished for centuries. Europeans—and Philip Wylie—even say that America is a matriarchy in which the dominance of women is simply expressed in covert ways.

Do girls hate technical subjects and boys love them? Not necessarily innately. Girls get dolls. Boys get Erector sets. No wonder the girls often dislike the angularities of ruler and compass later. I do not know what toys the Russians give their girl children, but it is said that most of their doctors and 30 per cent of their scientists are women, a fraction many times greater than in America. Their excess of scientists and engineers over ours is due to these numbers of women.

But I can mention two fields, music and poetry, where there is roughly equal social opportunity for both sexes to show their abilities and where real differences still seem to appear. Who takes the most music lessons in America? Girls. Which sex predominates in teaching music? Women. Up through high school there are plenty of girls in the school orchestras. A woman composer would not be frowned upon.

But who plays the piano spontaneously in the Student Union lounge? Always boys. Among adults, which sex composes? Which sex most often gets together for chamber music? Men. I would be glad to be convinced otherwise, but it seems to me that women may not have the musical vocation, except for a talented few.

Likewise in poetry. There are women poets, and good ones. I do not think they give the reader the sense of mastery; perhaps "mistressy" would describe it better. But today I see no discrimination, either by publishers or readers, against women authors, who are legion; yet the number of serious women poets is very much less than the number of men. *Gone with the Wind* is a good feminine *War and Peace*. Where is the good feminine Shakespeare or Milton?

I admire intellectual women. They represent a source of power that is kept under wraps in our society by our romantic ideas of work and marriage. The power is frittered away in bridge and benefits when it might have revolutionized medicine and remade cities. But even if they were released from these invisible chains, I think the women who have a real vocation for abstract creation might still be rare.

The male dominance in these fields resembles somewhat the male dominance in certain hereditary disorders, such as color blindness and hemophilia, which women sometimes do have, but much less frequently. Such disorders are said to be due to a sex-linked recessive gene. I have a whimsical notion that the male brilliance in abstract creation may be a sex-linked recessive disorder of the mind. The genetic make-up of women may tend to stabilize them against this disease and make them prin-

"I have a whimsical notion that the male brilliance in abstract creation may be a sex-linked recessive disorder of the mind."

cipally "carriers" of it, just as they are of color blindness.

Of course today we know that genetics is just the beginning of the difference between the sexes. The concentration of certain drugs in the body can strongly affect mental behavior in various ways, but the sex hormones are particularly powerful. Rats, male or female, injected with a trace of male hormone at a certain spot in the brain, come out fighting; with a trace of female hormone at another spot, they want to mother everything in sight. The survival of the species must often have depended on this sensitivity to our internal chemical balance. When such questions are better understood, we may come to know what are the "normal" mental and behavioral differences between the chemistries of the sexes, and how they vary with the changes in our bodies during growth and old age. Someday, even a "masculine" interest in abstract creation may be turned on and off like a faucet by taking the proper hormone.

The second big difference between human minds is far more obvious than the sexual differences, but it is harder to discuss because many of its more personal aspects are—and perhaps should be—socially taboo. Yet I think it is time for scientists and others to say aloud bluntly and clearly their various views on this matter, because our success as a democracy and indeed many aspects of our future welfare and happiness now depend on understanding it correctly.

The dreadful secret is that men differ greatly in intelligence. We all know this, of course, in a general way. You are not an Einstein and neither am I. Many of us have taken the tests and have found out our own intelligence quotients, or our children's. Naturally they make our blood pressure rise, and we are sure the tests are wrong—whether they show us to be feebleminded 80's or average 100's or managerial 130's. You cannot go around comparing IQs with your friends and fellow workers, unless you want to lose them all. This is why the subject is tricky to discuss.

As a result, many psychologists today dislike using the IQ. They say it is somewhat uncertain, that it arouses these emotional reactions, and that it stresses verbal and mathematical problem-solving abilities and neglects other valuable abilities in a person; for example, the emotional sensitivity and imagination that are needed by writers and creative artists. Nevertheless, the things I have to say about problem-solving in our society will be understood best if we keep something like the IQ scale in mind. It is the only index in general use that measures even roughly the tremendous differences in the analytical mental abilities of students and men. These differences are the dominant fact of life in the physical sciences and, I think, in every area where analytical brilliance is important.

The IQ scale is so powerful because a small difference in problem-solving ability, amounting, say, to ten IQ points, or a year or so in mental age, makes a big difference—an "order-of-magnitude difference"—in the difficulty of problems that can be solved. I have on my desk an amusing pocket guide to the restaurants of New York, published for engineers, which lists, among other things, the estimated IQ of the waiters in each restaurant. And it is startling to realize, as you do when you use this guide, how much more pleasure there is in eating where the waiter has a normal IQ of 100, alert and competent, than where the service is at the 90 or 80 level, subnormal, with inattentive service and misunderstood orders.

And the IQ scale covers a vast range of these order-of-magnitude differences. An adult chimpanzee can solve mechanical problems about as well as a six-year-old child and might be assigned an IQ of around 40 if he were an adult human being. A moron would be around 70, an average person 100, a Ph.D. student 140, and Pasteur and Einstein 180 or over.

The importance of ten-point differences is just as striking at the 140 level or the 180 level as it is at the 100 level. The Ph.D. student can see order-of-magnitude differences in his professors that the man in the street might not see at all or might misinterpret. Science is not so different from rock-climbing, which I once took some lessons in. It was only after the class had learned to claw their way up an easy fourth-degree slope that they began to appreciate the real risks and the beautiful performance of the men on the sixth-degree overhang up above.

The first hard fact for society about such a scale as the IQ scale is that, just as in mountain climbing, there are certain problems which cannot be solved except by men of the very greatest abilities. To prove the germ theory of disease or to make the first atomic pile, you need to have

"To prove the germ theory of disease or to make the first atomic pile, you need to have a 180 mind around."

a 180 mind around. This is equally true in organic chemistry, in philosophy; also in statecraft; perhaps in music and poetry, and perhaps even in art, as the example of Leonardo suggests. It does no good to assemble dozens of 170's or hundreds of 160's for such problems, except on the chance that there may be a 180 hidden among them. Seventeen Jonsons and Popes will not make a Shakespeare. On any problems that demand analytical thought and creation, men who work closely together are sensitive to differences of three or four points in each other's abilities. On the great problems a difference of ten points in some ability that is very much like IQ is what makes the final difference between achieving a solution and achieving a muddle.

I think the Sherlock Holmes stories are some of the best descriptions in print of these differences in analytical skill at the higher levels. Sherlock is about 170, while the clumsy detective Lestrade is about a 140. (Sherlock's brother Mycroft, who can solve mysteries just by sitting and thinking about them, is evidently a 180.) Lestrade's mistakes are the 140 mistakes—premature generalization, failure to understand the nature of proof or what a crucial experiment is. He does have an inquiring mind, and energy; what he lacks is rigor of analysis. Lestrade has the motivation, but only Holmes has the insight to find the hidden little key that unlocks the door; and the insight can hardly be explained or communicated until after the proof is in.

One of the troubles in science is that there are twenty Lestrades messing up the footprints and confusing the evidence for every Holmes who goes back to fundamentals and straightens it out. In nuclear physics it has recently turned out that for ten years the best experiments on beta-decay have been either wrong or misleading. Not really Lestrade results, just the elusiveness of the wily Moriarty again; and they are on the track once more. But this field is lucky. Most fields have nothing but Lestrade results for decades at a time.

There is an apocryphal story physicists tell about the late John von Neumann—probably a 180—that shows the difference they feel between such really high-speed minds and those of ordinary brilliance. It seems that a psychologist brought Von Neumann the following problem. Two bicyclists are ten miles apart, each cycling toward the other at ten miles per hour. A fly starts from one cyclist's nose, flies off at twenty miles per hour to the other cyclist, then back to the first, and so on, until the cyclists meet. How far does the fly fly?

The psychologist, according to the story, was giving this problem to various physicists and mathematicians and trying to distinguish the one type of mind from the other by the kinds of solutions they gave. The mathematicians were supposed to take about one minute (!) to solve it, because they would figure out how far the fly went on each leg of the zigzag and then sum up this (infinite) series of legs to give the total distance flown. The physicists, however, were supposed to solve it much faster, in about fifteen seconds, because they would figure immediately that the cyclists would meet in half an hour, and in that time the fly at his speed would have flown just ten miles.

But when the problem was put to Von Neumann, he solved it in ten seconds! The psychologist said, "How is this? You're supposed to be primarily a mathematician, not a physicist! You should have summed the series and taken one minute, instead of using velocities and taking fifteen seconds." Von Neumann replied, "But I did sum the series!"

Psychologists have indeed been studying the mental processes of physical scientists lately, and with similarly baffling results. One psychologist reported seriously that half the physicists were antisocial because they didn't answer his letters, and that the other half were neurotic because they visualized Rorschach patterns in three dimensions! For this kind of Lestrade to be let loose on such a study is exactly as pathetic as for a subnormal waitress in the 90 range to try to measure the intellectual differences in college students.

Unfortunately, few of us are big enough or matter-of-fact enough not to be offended when a smart man shows he knows he is smart. I saw one nuclear physicist—a 180 analytically but perhaps something less in his social skills—antagonize a whole audience during a debate at a meeting, when he said bluntly, "I do not quarrel with third-rate scientists. I quarrel with first-rate scientists." One man said afterward, "What does he expect me to do—shoot myself?"

He was emotionally involved because he still thought of himself as competing. Twenty points lower down on the IQ scale and he would merely have been amused. Only a competing violinist could be envious of Heifetz. Only a competing basketball team would resent the height of the Harlem Globetrotters or expect them to be modest about it. When the intellectual levels are far enough apart, they can work at different kinds of problems, can serve each other and be served, appreciate and admire each other, without contempt or resentment. But there are many problems that a democracy can solve only when it is kept in mind that the difference in problem-solving ability between the mind of the good Pasteur and the lowest mind that can still be called human is as great as the difference between an average man and a chimpanzee.

The second hard fact about the IQ scale is that there are not very many brilliant men at the top of it. At the 190 level, which might describe Archimedes, Newton, and Gauss, we have been seeing about one every five hundred years. The recent increases in population and in the percentage of people who go into analytical fields will speed up the rate. (Ninety per cent of all the scientists who ever lived are living today.) At the 180 level there might be a dozen living Americans. This is the level, say, of Darwin, Freud, Shaw, Bertrand Russell, Percy Bridgman, Linus Pauling—name your own. By the time we get down to 170, there are some three hundred in the United States; at 160, about five thousand; at 150, about one hundred thousand; at 140, about one million.

"The difference . . . between the mind of the good Pasteur and the lowest mind that can still be called human is as great as the difference between an average man and a chimpanzee."

As soon as you say seriously that a man is one of the fifty or so brightest minds in the country—or one of any other number—you have placed him remarkably well on this scale. The smartest man in an average community of one thousand, or the brightest pupil in an average high school of this size, will be up in the 140's—Ph.D. material. Half a dozen or so in such a school are the ones we depend upon to make our scientists, engineers, and doctors.

Do many of these go unrecognized? It is true that some of the great ones have been slow in school. (Think how slow a human being would seem at chimpanzee lessons.) Every teacher imagines that one of his daydreamers is simply stepping to the music of a different drummer. But most of those who make their mark show some sign early and are picked for success. Some studies indicate that in America at least half of the white Protestant boys capable of getting Ph.D.'s in the physical sciences do get them. The 170's may get their Ph.D.'s as young as twenty-two or twenty-three, some three years earlier than the 140's, and they will have international reputations before they are thirty-five. There is no difficulty in spotting them, and teachers and patrons rush in to help them along.

What have these statistics to do with society? I claim that they show us a good deal about what we can expect of Congressmen, schoolteachers and schoolchildren, college students, and many other groups. Obviously we can always use more people at the top. The care with which we identify them early and help them find the great teachers they need and deserve, is what governs our ability to win Nobel prizes, to find cures for cancer and schizophrenia, and to make rockets and radar.

But what about the people below the top? For example, the question is often raised whether Congress is really stupid or only acts that way. The answer is that IQ estimates from their educational records and occupations show that as a group

Congressmen are pretty smart, mostly in the 130's and above. This is the range where some psychologists say we find maximum leadership. Einstein is supposed to have said that the trouble with chemists is that chemistry is too hard for them. If our representatives collectively have trouble knowing what to do about national and international problems, it is not because they are individually stupid; it is because these problems are almost impossibly hard for them or for anyone else.

What about teachers? In our present educational setup we need about one of them per thirty pupils, or one per hundred of the whole population. This means some two million teachers. If we took every woman over 130 for this job, we would barely have this number. It is therefore one of the facts of life that teachers will generally have IQs in the 120 range. This means that most will be unable to graduate from very good colleges, and so the notoriously poor quality of teachers colleges is almost a necessary evil. Leading citizens—in the 130 range themselves—will be contemptuous of such teachers, and bright children of thirteen or fourteen —the 130's and 140's—will already know more in certain subjects than most of their teachers. There is no remedy for it, except, first, to help bright children get the very best teachers and the best outside help to enlarge their horizons. (If the intellectuals each took on one protégé to enrich, it would be worth dozens of alarm meetings.) And second, to use more educational television and movies, so that the most brilliant of the teachers can reach thousands or millions of students at a time.

"Teachers will generally have IQs in the 120 range. . . . bright children of thirteen or fourteen will know more than most of their teachers."

Or look at the children. The central problem of mass education is that half of the children are subnormal. By definition. This country has done one of the finest things in the world in extending education for the whole population to age eighteen; but we must not then expect them all to master the Latin and algebra and physics that were suited to the top 5 per cent in the year 1900. In a democracy, with this great range of intellectual abilities, I think that equality of opportunity demands a separate kind of education for each level of ability. We must make a system where we can challenge every student to his limit. But we must challenge him in the range of his own abilities, not in the range of someone else's abilities.

We may be beginning to get larger numbers of people at the top as a result of our strong intellectual selection in marriage.

It is all the result of coeducation. The smartest 10 per cent of our young people, the 120's and 130's, are selected and thrown together at the most susceptible age for romance. About half the college men marry college women. Almost all college women marry college men or, alas, remain unmarried.

This is preference, not just propinquity. I sometimes suspect that intelligence, smell, and politics are what really determine our choice of a mate. Dimwits, garlic-eaters, and do-nothings must marry one another. It gives them the reassuring atmosphere of home. I think that close friendships and free marriages do not often bridge an IQ gap of more than twenty points.

And these college marriages produce bright children. It is not certain whether the intelligence of a child is more a matter of inheritance or of early stimulation, although some psychologists now suspect the latter. But whatever the explanation is, it looks today as if the children of the college marriages are clustering about the average of their parents' abilities, scattering above and below in much the same way that children of unselected parents scatter above and below the average of the whole population. If this proves to be so, it has the remarkable consequence that these marriages are now producing *five or ten times* the total number of 150's, for example, that we would get from perfectly random marriages in the normal population.

Even more spectacular children may be coming out of the intellectual colonies like Oak Ridge or Los Alamos, where one man in six has a Ph.D.; or the faculty communities of the great universities, where all the men and many of the women have advanced degrees. Collectively these communities really form a small town of twenty thousand people or so, with the Ph.D.'s moving around from one colony to another as frequently as Du Pont branch managers. They all know each other, more or less, and large social circles of 130's and 140's spring up in such centers. When the children go to a common—or uncommon—school, whole classes of 130's and 140's may be seen, from kindergarten through high school.

In the general population, with an average IQ of 100, only one person in three hundred reaches the 140 level. But in communities with an average of 140, does one child in three hundred reach 180? And one in two thousand reach 190? If this turns out to be so, we may not have to wait centuries for the next Newton; we may have a dozen Newtons within twenty years. The number of 180's getting out of college in the next few years may not be a mere dozen, but hundreds. It could be an explosion of genius such as the world has never seen.

I actually think I see some of these real geniuses sprouting around me today. A thirteen-year-old is studying atomic physics seriously; an eleven-year-old is taking college courses; an eight-year-old is doing graduate work in mathematics. Even in a university community they are frightening—and wonderful. How do we root and shield them, and yet challenge and educate them for civic and world responsibility? That is the most important problem for their parents and perhaps also for the nation. If I am right about this crop, it is not far from the mark to speak of a new race of men.

In fact these intellectual communities are just one by-product of the general organization and maximization of intellectual development that is the central achievement of our century. All our other achievements really flow from this one. It is a kind of forced draft of the intellect. From grade school all through life we stimulate individuals to excel, praise and reward them for it, and select the excellent for further challenges. We have organizations, industrial and governmental, to program invention and discovery, and to make them easier by breaking them down into consecutive steps that even little men can solve. Yet while the labor is reduced, the talent to do it is continually stimulated by stirring the fire. The old molds of place, hierarchy, and custom that once permitted a man to stagnate after the age of thirty, are broken and broken again for our mobile scientists and managers. Intellectual communities spring up to house this constant flux of brilliance. These centers of research and learning interact with every aspect of American life from the Iowa farms to Cape Canaveral.

It all forms an intellectual furnace such as the world has never seen. Compared to this, mankind has never used its brains before. And I see new brains coming into service.

Thoreau said, as though he had looked at our statistics:

The millions are awake enough for physical labor; but only one in a million is awake enough for effective intellectual exertion, only one in a hundred millions to a poetic or divine life. To be awake is to be alive. I have never yet met a man who was quite awake.

He was talking about something more like renunciation and insight than science, but at this level of dedication the distinction almost disappears. He would have liked to meet the men awakening today.

Once we have begun to appreciate the heights and depths of human intellectual achievement, we can go on to explore the diverse directions that achievement takes. It seems to me that brilliance is naturally differentiated into two or three specialties. The classes that strike me most strongly as natural ones are the musicians, the poets, the mathematicians, and perhaps the painters. The IQ is probably not a good enough index for classifying such diverse abilities; perhaps we ought to think of a more generalized "talent index" or TQ. Nevertheless, two things are remarkable about the specialties I have just listed: first, that the brilliant youngsters may show their talent in these directions at a very early age; and second, that they may tend to marry each other not only by degree of talent but by specialty.

Who can produce, before he is twenty-one, a masterwork that the whole world will appreciate for generations? Anne Frank, perhaps, but it is her circumstances and her innocence that touch us rather than genius. But there are many musicians: Mozart, composing at six; Mozart and Bizet, writing symphonies at seventeen that we still enjoy. There are poets: Keats and Shelley. And some mathematicians: Abel and Galois were dead almost before they were men.

What is peculiar about these fields? We would not trust a judge or a doctor or a philosopher aged six—or aged seventeen, either. The answer is obvious: omission of the external world. These are the abstract fields, the fields of almost purely formal manipulation of symbols into patterns—musical symbols, verbal symbols, mathematical symbols.

In fields requiring more human experience, beyond mere logic, success comes later and later. The Nobel prizes in physics and chemistry generally go to men in their thirties, and in medicine to men in their forties; in law and philosophy any similar achievements come first in the fifties and sixties. Even in the formal fields, works achieved under twenty are not the greatest of a creator's life. It takes more than just symbols, it takes external reference and understanding to move us deeply. But the symbolic manipulations are a sign of intellectual power.

The second peculiarity of these natural fields of brilliance is that of inbreeding. It is most obvious in the musicians. America now has more symphony orchestras, more chamber music, a larger total attendance at concerts, and so on, than any other country. Adding up all the serious musicians in this crowd—say the ones who practice once a day or join a group to play or sing once a week—we may have 10 per cent or more of the adult population. And they marry each other. They meet over the piano. They want music in the home. They go in clusters to Interlochen or Aspen or the Berkshire Festival, romance no objection, to form musical colonies more single-minded, even if shorter-lived, than the intellectual colonies I spoke of earlier. My guess is that well over half the time the seriously musical marry others in the clan, an inbreeding at least as strong as that in the coeducational colleges.

Why is this more significant than that people who like dancing or bowling should marry one another? Or office employees? As of course they do, in much the same selective way. It is more significant because of the evidence we have seen that the musical mind may be a special type of mind. Aside from the question discussed earlier of masculine dominance in musical creation, the musical mind may be—may be, I emphasize—another genetic trait that only pops up in a few per cent of the population, like red hair. If it is, inbreeding among musicians could produce a group of people less and less like the nonmusical, as inbreeding is said to have produced in Scotland and Ireland whole villages of redheaded people.

Much the same is true, though to a smaller degree, among poets and writers. They have their classes and conferences, too, where the sexes meet in an atmosphere of respect and sympathy. The English instructor doesn't marry the beautiful nurse; he marries the lit major who knows what he is talking about. I cannot say whether the same is true of mathematicians; they are so

"The English instructor doesn't marry the beautiful nurse; he marries the lit major who knows what he is talking about."

few in number, and the girl mathematicians are fewer still. But in physics, the next field over, up to half of the girl graduate students may marry physical scientists.

But whether brilliance in these arts will be inherited or only acquired, the colonies and concentrations of specialists may be taking the human race in new directions. As geographical isolation breaks down, the great historical races of man, with their so obvious external animal differences of noses and skin, are amalgamating on a hundred fronts. The internal differences, however, the differences of sheer intellect and of various kinds of abstract creativity, may be diverging into new races of mind, all Newtons, Beethovens, and Michelangelos, as far removed from what we have called normal as what we have called normal is removed from the gorilla.

What symphonies they will compose! What laws they will discover! What centuries lie ahead!

John Rader Platt is currently Visiting Professor in Biology at M.I.T., although his home campus is the University of Chicago. This article will appear in his new book The Excitement of Science *(Houghton Mifflin), which also includes the article that he wrote for* HORIZON *on "The Fifth Need of Man" (July, 1959).*

HAYDN

A Presence More Vivid than Ever

During thirty of his most productive winters, while Kapellmeister to the Princes Esterházy, Haydn composed in these rooms in his house at Eisenstadt, southeast of Vienna. In charge of the abundant musical life at the nearby palace and at Esterháza, his patrons' summer residence, Haydn trained and conducted a staff of singers and instrumentalists (performing in colorful livery like the coat shown here) and wrote for them an enormous amount of superb music. The autograph of a string quartet and the libretto to one of his operas are on the table. In rare free minutes he may have practiced violin beside the stove in the next room.

The Haydn renaissance, a major musical phenomenon of our time, continues to astonish music lovers and to baffle the experts. In the past twenty-five years, more of Haydn's music has been performed than was performed during the entire preceding century. All over the world, wherever the classical music of the West is admired, new enthusiasts are beginning to discover unexpected depths and delights in the music of Joseph Haydn.

In Vienna all of Haydn's symphonies are now being recorded; half of them have never been performed since Haydn died. A hard-boiled musical observer calls the recording sessions "a series of fantastic experiences." Many of the orchestra members who grew up assuming that they knew all about Haydn are astonished at the wealth of great music which they have never played before. "Every day they make new and exciting discoveries. Over a hundred symphonies and not two of them alike."

Much of the Haydn revival has been made possible by high fidelity and the long-playing record. Where once the repertory was confined to the tired war horses, now we hear concertos and divertimentos by the dozens from hitherto unheard-of composers. Where Haydn was once known to the average concert-goer for a few quartets and symphonies, now anyone can know him for trios, masses, and operas of which only scholars were formerly aware. With the greater sophistication of the listeners has come a greater sophistication of performance. No longer are we content with music of the classical period played as a simple, light-weight, geometrical game; we expect the musicians to express, within the terms of the style, the same intensity of feeling that the composers put into it.

Haydn is still the least familiar among the world's great composers. No complete edition of his works exists. The first authentic scores of his twelve London symphonies are now being printed. Of his operas some are being published for the first time. If all goes well, everything of major significance that Haydn wrote will be published within the next three years.

Haydn lived to the age of seventy-seven, composed almost every day, and left an astonishing quantity of work. No one knows exactly how much—a hundred and four symphonies, eighty-four string quartets (the last of them was discovered as late as 1931), fifty-two piano sonatas, at least twenty concertos for various instruments, twenty-four operas and *Singspiele*, fourteen masses, thirty-one trios for piano and strings, more than two hundred divertimentos for chamber ensembles, about a hundred and seventy-five pieces for baryton (a species of viol played by Haydn's great patron, Prince Nikolaus Esterházy, "the Magnificent"). And this list is by no means complete. Some major works by Haydn are believed to

Photographs ERICH LESSING

By JOSEPH WECHSBERG

be still buried in the archives of castles and monasteries in Czechoslovakia, Hungary, and Rumania.

Haydn the man is emerging from obscurity along with Haydn the artist. The popular, patronizing myth of "Papa Haydn" as a somewhat genial, innocuous patriarch has been completely dispelled by the discoveries of the past fifty years. We know today that Haydn was a complex personality who led more than one life, and had an unsuspected range of inner feeling.

Both the music and the man were revolutionary. True, even in his revolutionary moods Haydn remains gentle and genial, a genuine Austrian. His outward gracefulness conceals his inner boldness. Yet this seemingly contented gentleman, the conciliatory conductor, the helpful friend of younger composers, was the same Haydn who broke with hallowed traditions and created new musical forms. The rebellious spirit appears unexpectedly; suddenly there are haunting harmonies, such as in the first movement of his wonderful String Quartet in C (Opus 74, No. 1) where he uses chromatic innovations which must have come as a shock and a revelation to his contemporaries. He was the inventor of the string quartet as we know it today.

Haydn's rebellion against authority was never as obvious as Beethoven's. He expressed his opposition more deftly but just as firmly. During the long, "dark" period of his life he spent thirty years as *Kapellmeister* of the princely household orchestra at Esterházy Castle in Eisenstadt (now the capital of Austria's Burgenland province). His patron, Nikolaus, expected profound submission from his personnel. Once in a while he thought he had to economize and intended to dismiss a member of the orchestra. Whereupon *Kapellmeister* Haydn (who hated to write letters) would sit down, draw the sign of the Cross, and patiently write to his "Serene Highness and Noble Prince of the Holy Roman Empire, Gracious and Dread Lord." In every case we know of, Haydn seems to have had his way. As time went on he became stronger and the Prince more mellow. Instead of writing directly, Haydn would ask the Princely Secretary Scheffstoss to act as intermediary. Later he became bolder still and asked for personal interviews with the Prince—a method he found far more effective.

Haydn and his musicians hated the "desert"—the icy marshes of Esterháza, twenty-five miles from Eisenstadt—

The most brilliant of Haydn's many achievements as a composer are his symphonies. He wrote no less than 104, and most of them were first performed in this splendid baroque hall in the Esterházy palace at Eisenstadt. Experimenting with his small orchestra—whose chairs are represented here as at the end of the "Farewell" Symphony, in which the players depart one by one—Haydn converted the symphonic form into an unsurpassed medium of instrumental expression.

where the Prince had built himself another castle, "to rival Versailles," with an opera house for four hundred people, a theatre, a coffeehouse, a frescoed hall, a picture gallery, a library, and terraces, parks, cascades, vistas. In 1772, when Haydn and his musicians were particularly lonely for the warmth of Eisenstadt and the gaiety of Vienna, Haydn wrote his "Farewell" Symphony (No. 45, in F-sharp minor). The orchestra played it for the Prince. During the final movement one musician after another blew out the candle on his music rack and tiptoed away until only the first and second violinists were left. "The beautiful and lonely symphony succeeded far better than any letter could have done," writes H. C. Robbins Landon, the eminent Haydn scholar. The Prince took the hint and gave orders to return to Eisenstadt.

Outwardly Haydn seemed to blend readily into the landscape of his time. *Kapellmeister* Haydn had to wear the princely household uniform—blue and gold, with white stockings—at Esterházy Castle, and he was often treated like a lackey. He was obliged to perform two operas and two concerts a week with his court orchestra, rehearse the musi-cians and coach the singers, and prepare the music for religious services. Each morning he had to present himself in the Prince's antechamber and ask what His Highness wished him to compose. It was not an easy life, but we may at least reflect that Prince Esterházy would have been forgotten long since if he had not been Haydn's employer.

By the time Haydn returned to Vienna in 1795, after his second triumphant visit to London, he was a celebrity, the most renowned composer in Europe. As the retainer of another Esterházy, the despotic Prince Nikolaus II, a grandson of his erstwhile patron, he was no longer willing to behave like a lackey. Once the Prince walked into a rehearsal and made some criticism. Haydn gave him a cool stare. "That, Your Highness," he said, "is my affair." "The Prince," reports Mr. Landon, "white with fury, turned on his heel and left the room." Fortunately his wife had more sense. When relations between Haydn and her husband became particularly strained, she would reconcile the two. Gradually the despotic prince changed his ways.

Haydn had courage, wit, and irony. He dared write to the

By 1792 Haydn, home from a triumphant visit to England, was the most celebrated composer in Europe. Late that year young Beethoven came to study with him. In a letter (right) Beethoven's friend Count Waldstein urged the young man to work diligently so as to "receive the spirit of Mozart"—whose death the previous year had grieved both Haydn and Beethoven— "from the hands of Haydn." But eminent master and arrogant pupil, despite their respect for one another as composers, clashed temperamentally; Haydn liked to refer to Beethoven jokingly as "that Great Mogul." Although Haydn was retained and paid by the Esterházys till his death in 1809, he now lived and worked independently in Vienna, traveling occasionally by coach to Eisenstadt or Esterháza by way of Forchtenstein (opposite), one of his patrons' residences.

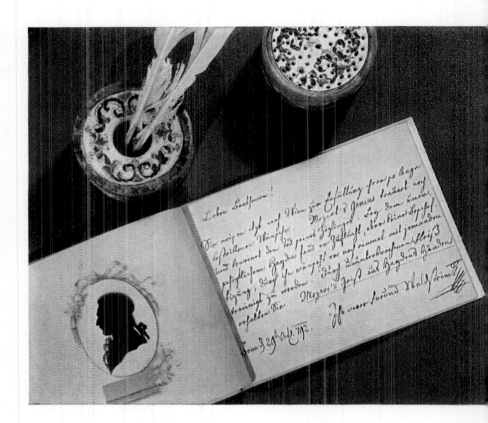

powerful Elector of Cologne on behalf of his pupil Beethoven, who would "in time fill the position of one of Europe's greatest composers." The letter is a masterpiece of sardonic innuendo. Haydn openly reprimands the mighty *Kurfürst* for his stinginess. "Undoubtedly Your Highness had his reasons for choosing to send [Beethoven] into the great world with such a paltry sum." The Elector, needless to say, was not pleased.

In dealing with his music publishers Haydn was a shrewd businessman. There were no copyright laws at the time: copyists could bribe orchestra members to let them copy a new work, which they would then sell on their own. For years Haydn watched with growing irritation all the music being published under his name in Paris, London, Berlin, and Amsterdam, for which he got nothing at all. Finally he got tough with the publishers. To Artaria & Company in Vienna he wrote, "In order to compose your 3 pianoforte Sonatas particularly well, I had to buy a new fortepiano. Now since no doubt you have long since realized that scholars are sometimes short of money—and that is my situation

at present—I should like to ask you . . . to pay 31 gold ducats to the organ and instrument-maker Wenzl Schanz. . . . I don't like to be in debt to tradesmen but since . . . great people keep me waiting so long for payment, things have come to a standstill." Another time Haydn complains, "It is always painful for me to note that not a single work of mine that you have published is free from errors."

The notebooks of Haydn's journeys to England reveal him as a shrewd and understanding observer. He was shocked by the local drinking habits and by the "miserable trash" performed at the English opera. As in Vienna, he soon had a wide circle of acquaintances, ranging from the Prince of Wales to Mister March, "dentist, *Carossieur* [coachmaker], and dealer in wines." Haydn's interests were as divergent as his company and his curiosity as invariable as his sense of humor. On one page he writes about his compositions and on the next about a recipe "to preserve cream and milk for a long time." He writes that "at the beginning of May 1792, Lord Barrymore gave a ball that cost 5,000 guineas. He paid 1,000 guineas for 1,000 peaches.

81

After long seclusion caused by failing health, Haydn appeared in public for the last time at the old University in Vienna (opposite) in March, 1808, a year before his death. The occasion, announced on the poster to be seen beside the door, was a performance of his oratorio The Creation, *to celebrate his seventy-sixth birthday. A great crowd cheered Haydn when he arrived in the Esterházy carriage; too frail to ascend to the hall, he was carried in a chair resembling that in the foreground, amid flourishes of trumpets and drums. During the performance he became so agitated that he had to be taken home. Tearful admirers embraced him as he left, and Beethoven kissed his hands.*

2,000 baskets of gusberes [gooseberries], 5 shillings a basket." We are told that "in France the girls are virtuous and the wives are whores; in Holland the girls are whores and the wives are virtuous; in England they stay proper all their lives." In a cynical mood Haydn reports that "if anybody steals £2 he is hanged; but if I trust anybody with £2,000 and he carries it off to the devil, he is acquitted." Nothing escaped him. He reports, "Milord Chatam [*sic*], President [*sic*] of the War Office and brother of Minister Pitt, was so drunk for 3 days he couldn't even sign his name, and thus occasioned that Lord Howe couldn't leave London, and together with the whole fleet couldn't sail away."

Haydn was an enthusiastic traveler. His marriage was very unhappy, and he was glad to get away from his nagging wife. In London—he was almost sixty then—he fell very much in love with Rebecca Schroeter, that mysterious lady of London society, whose husband, J. C. Bach's successor as Master of the Queen's Music, had died in 1788. Mrs. Schroeter wrote Haydn, "No language can express half the love and affection I feel for you, you are dearer to me every day of my life." And we know of course that earlier in his life Haydn had had an ardent love affair with Luigia Polzelli, a mediocre mezzo-soprano with a graceful figure. "Oh, my dear Polzelli," he wrote her, "you are always in my heart, and I shall never, never forget you."

Haydn worked long and hard on his compositions, though you would never think so to hear the exhilarating freshness of his music. In his later years he would begin right after breakfast, playing the harpsichord to get himself in the mood. He would sketch until lunch and, after a walk, start work again at four in the afternoon, when he did most of his scoring. He would continue until eight, take another short walk, and compose for an hour before going to bed. It took him a month to write a mass. Needless to say he did not know he was writing masterpieces; he accepted commissions and did the best he could, as an artist and a craftsman.

This complex, enigmatic man loved the folk melodies and popular songs of his native land. He often listened to the gypsies from Hungary, to their rhythms and syncopations; and he used Hungarian, Croatian, or Slavic melodies in the minuets or fast movements of his chamber music and symphonies. In one of his earlier quartets, Opus 20, No. 4, he writes an allegretto *alla zingarese;* and the wonderful presto of Opus 33, No. 3, has the sort of czardas melody that would make anyone want to dance.

Haydn wrote with his intellect as well as with his heart. He was an optimist, a deeply religious man, warm and compassionate, who believed there would be peace after war and happiness after sorrow. He had his melancholy moments: in 1791 he wrote to Mme Polzelli, "For quite some time now I have had days of depression without really knowing why . . ." but in his heart this friendliest of the great composers believed in the eternal happiness of life and love, in the beauty of nature, the taste of good wine, the sound of laughter. Haydn leaves us with an aftertaste of cheerfulness. The inner tension is always resolved into a happy ending, as with no other great composer. There are moments of deep melancholy in Haydn's music, but never the all-pervading gloom of Beethoven. Haydn's zest for life is infectious.

To every time its own music: Haydn's is God's gift to our own. In this age of anxiety people still come out of a concert hall, after a performance of Haydn's *The Creation* or *The Seasons,* smiling, exhilarated, excited. They seem to feel like the Italian musician on Saint Anne's Day of 1799, who walked into St. Michael's Church in Vienna a sick man to listen to one of Haydn's masses. "I perspired during the Credo and was terribly sick, but then my headache went away, and I felt cured mentally and physically," he wrote. Today Haydn's therapeutic powers are greater than ever.

Haydn himself explained the secret of his music and his artistic creed one day in 1802, after the members of the *Musikverein* in Bergen on the Baltic island of Rügen sent him a flattering letter. Haydn wrote back, "You reassure me . . . that I am often the enviable means by which you, and so many other families sensible of heartfelt emotion, derive, in their homely circle, their pleasure—their enjoyment. How reassuring is this thought to me! Often . . . a secret voice whispered to me: 'There are so few happy and contented people here below; grief and sorrow are always their lot; perhaps your labors will once be a source from which the care-worn, or the man burdened with affairs, can derive a few moments' rest and refreshment.'"

A resident of Vienna, Joseph Wechsberg often writes on musical subjects for HORIZON. *He is author of* Red Plush and Black Velvet, *a recent biography of soprano Nellie Melba.*

In Print: JOHN UPDIKE

"They were just people, members of the race of white animals. . . . Highly neural, brachycephalic, uniquely able to oppose their thumbs to the four other digits, they bred within elegant settlements, and both burned and interred their dead."

They are the people of John Updike's world. Rootless but insidiously regimented, they live "as cells do in the coffin, for the conception 'America' had died in their skulls." They come, for the most part, from the small cities of Pennsylvania and New England, and they have "an instinctive taste for the small appliances of civilization, the little grinders and slicers and holders." If they are not young—in their teens or early twenties—they are often old; but whether they are young or old, they suffer in whispers inner torments and defeats as acutely observed, as moving and as oppressive as any in modern American fiction. And occasionally they run.

Their creator knows them—in motion or repose—as litmus knows acid or silver knows light. There is in John Updike's writing the kind of visceral understanding that can whiten a world to being in the flicker of a phrase or in a sudden crackle of speech. Mr. Updike knows, for instance, about the ominous quiet of a "Sunday-stunned town," or the unctuous and barren comforts of the "progressive" church ("If there's to be a true healing it must be Harry and Janice who act"), or just how it is with an old man when, as "moisture walks out from his mouth," he lights a cigar. He understands—better than foundries of sociological discourse can ever understand—the arcane folk rituals of adolescence (on the orchard-dappled plains of central New Jersey, we are told, the older boys and girls parade nude in the headlights of their cars). And because John Updike writes of a more representative American experience, he tells us something other than what that fellow chronicler of the young, J. D. Salinger, tells us. For if Salinger reflects what the young would like to be, Updike tells us what they are.

He does so, he insists, by accident. John Updike believes that "a writer's business is not to write about his own time" but to express "the correct complexity and ambiguity of life." If he finds his ambiguities in the young and old, it is because "they are the people I know; I don't feel qualified to write about the middle-aged." Now thirty, Updike grew up in Shillington, Pennsylvania, the only child of a high-school mathematics teacher, and he feels that the geographical accident of his birth—until he was eighteen and

went to Harvard he had little experience of cities—perhaps made him "a kind of throwback" to an earlier, less urban America. The additional accident of age exempted Mr. Updike from the wars and imposed on him a "rather quiet" life: a year's postgraduate study (drawing) at Oxford, two years as a staff writer for *The New Yorker,* followed by withdrawal with his wife and three children to Ipswich, Massachusetts, a handsomely antiquated town from which he has launched several dozen short stories and the second of his two novels, *Rabbit, Run.*

Recently, in a review of a book by Salinger, Updike wrote what can stand as a general prescription for his own work: "As Hemingway sought the words for things in motion, Salinger seeks the words for things transmuted into human subjectivity. . . . Few writers since Joyce would risk such a wealth of words upon events that are purely internal and deeds that are purely talk." Updike's deeds are not purely talk, but it is true that his is an inner-directed eye and that his tales move forward not in a crescendo of climaxes but by the slow accretion of small and apparently random detail. In his first novel, *The Poorhouse Fair,* a remarkable evocation of the terrors and triumphs of old age (John Updike grew up with two grandparents), the "plot" has to do with the revolt of the inmates of a poor farm. Totally unpremeditated, it grows like a malignant vine—a Pepsi-Cola truck rams a wall, rain falls, four old men share a pint of rye, revolt comes in a shower of stones directed at the Prefect's retreating back. In *Rabbit, Run* a former high-school basketball star comes home to find his pregnant wife drunk before the television set; the living room is littered with toys, his wife is out of cigarettes, the car has been left with his mother-in-law—and the rabbit runs.

For all the apparent poverty of their surfaces, both novels send their roots deep—to the place where a true moral dialectic begins. And over both novels, indeed, over much of Updike's work, hangs something else—some pervasive sense of loss. Visitors to the poor home sense it, and the hero of *Rabbit, Run* is haunted by it when he longs to drive "right into the broad soft belly of the land, surprising the dawn cottonfields with his northern plates." They are looking for a simpler, more virtuous land, for an America that eroded with the frontier. Will they find it? Updike, who does not "wish my fiction to be any clearer than life," cannot know—or care. What matters is that they—and the man who is their understanding—continue to try.

RICHARD W. MURPHY

84

On Stage: MAUREEN FORRESTER

Six years ago a handsome, wholesome woman of Valkyrian proportions walked onto the stage of New York's Town Hall. She was virtually unknown, the audience was small, and, as often happens at New York debuts, most of the listeners had got their tickets for nothing and expected nothing much in return. Then Maureen Forrester began to sing. Within five minutes the walls of the auditorium seemed to turn iridescent, and the air was colored by a voice which the next day's critics would compare to the luminosity of a stained-glass window.

They had every right to do so, for the circumstances of Miss Forrester's voice are rare. She is, to begin with, a contralto, a *real* contralto, with a virtuosity and beauty that extend to the lowest notes of her register. Today a whole regiment of singers claim the distinctions of the contralto range. Many of these claims are false. Mostly they are made by mezzo-sopranos, that is to say, sopranos with a handful of lower notes they dredge up for special occasions. But they do not possess the depth, warmth, richness, and ripeness of the true contralto, who is in effect a "female baritone."

Unlike some self-styled contraltos, who sound like bellowing moose impaled on a fence, Miss Forrester has never released a note that is not all velvet. At the age of thirty-one she has already sung with every leading conductor in this country. Her voice is at home in seven lands and languages; her German diction, in particular, is accurate to the last umlaut, as audiences in the Central Europe of Mahler, Schubert, Schumann, and Wolf have discovered.

But for all her fame, she is not one of those prima donnas given to outbursts and tantrums that quiver the hardiest accompanist or conductor; and her colleagues claim that she is so even-tempered that she has no right to be as good a singer as she is. Her home life, between concert tours, is equally undramatic. She avoids elaborate socializing, feeling no need to impress people when she is off stage.

Born and reared in Canada, Maureen Forrester studied singing as a young girl and then, to her surprise, her voice changed when she was sixteen, rather as a boy's does at a slightly earlier age. Within a month she developed into a contralto, a condition that might have proved something of a disaster, since good opera parts for contraltos are few and not always rewarding; a number of them, as in Gluck's *Orfeo*, represent male roles. As Miss Forrester puts it with her usual bluntness, "In opera, contraltos are either mothers, maids, witches, or bitches—the only part I'd fit is that of a mother. I've had four children in the last six years, so I do know something about them. Still, I intend to get involved in opera some day."

She already has more than enough qualifications for an operatic career but is waiting for the propitious moment. In the meantime she has made her reputation as a lieder singer. From song to song, from performance to performance, her recitals are as carefully delivered as her recordings—of which the most celebrated are those of Mahler's *Kindertotenlieder* and *Song of the Earth*. Her training as a church singer prepared her for sacred music, too, especially Bach.

Yet, like all conscientious artists, she is never satisfied with her standards, and is still, in one sense, a student, even though her schedule is so packed that she has almost no time to practice: each performance serves as her rehearsal-and-warming-up session for the next concert. Whenever she returns to Montreal, she takes up her studies with the baritone Bernard Diamant. She also turns to her husband, Eugene Kash, a Canadian violinist and conductor, for advice whenever she confronts an artistic problem too vexing for her to handle alone. "It doesn't happen often," she will tell you, "but when it does, Eugene is the genius, not me."

To date, the Forrester history is a Cinderella story come to life. At the moment she is the reigning queen of the contralto world and, in the view of many critics, there are no successors in sight. According to Miss Forrester, though, great singers are trained, not born, and not unexpectedly, she herself would like to teach in a few years.

"I will show my pupils how to create a song performance," she says, "not only sing it. First they must learn the words, learn every detail of what they mean. Then they must become comfortable with the rhythm of the piece, even if it means beating out that rhythm while they are traveling on a plane or train from one engagement to another. Only after that, when you know everything there is to know about a lied, do you start on the melody. And while you are studying the melody—the flow of the vocal line—you have to watch carefully for the spots where you will have technical difficulties. From there, you work on those tricky places—when you conquer them, you are ready to appear before the public. I want to pass along all the things experience has taught me, because I'm perfectly sure I'll be able to turn out better singers than I am."

Better singers? The statement is surprising, coming as it does from a throat that has poured out contralto song as opulent as that of Schumann-Heink, Louise Homer, Ebe Stignani, Kathleen Ferrier, Bruna Castagna, or Sigrid Onegin. Certainly, it would be an impressive feat if Miss Forrester could communicate her technique to other singers. But today's audiences are more than satisfied to hear Maureen Forrester in the original.   JAY HARRISON

The Judgments of Joan

Her trial and execution were
only the beginning. In the
centuries since, the Maid has
continued to provoke anger
and adoration, skepticism and awe

*Joan's portrait in miniature, believed to
be a good likeness, was painted by an
unknown fifteenth-century Franco-Flemish
artist and appears in a manuscript of
poems by Charles D'Orléans. The text that
follows is adapted from Mr. Lightbody's
book on the fluctuations in Joan's
fame, to be published in the United States
by the Harvard University Press.*

By CHARLES WAYLAND LIGHTBODY

"You have heard the last of her," says the Executioner to the Earl of Warwick in George Bernard Shaw's play *Saint Joan;* to which pious reassurance Warwick responds, with wise caution: "The last of her? Hm! I wonder!" In a later scene, the Executioner himself admits his failure: "I could not kill the Maid. She is up and alive everywhere.'

After the lapse of more than five centuries, every detail of her life, her visions, and her achievement remains significant to countless numbers of our contemporaries. This peasant girl who never got out of her teens, who had an active career of little more than two years, whose life ended in heroic martyrdom at an age when girls today leave school—this peasant girl left such an impress upon the history of her time that many members of each succeeding generation of Western civilized men have thought it worthwhile to record, often at full length, their varied comments upon her in countless histories and biographies, dramas, poems, pictures, and works of music. Her trial has been described as "a trial that has become second in importance only to the trial of Christ." She has had, in fact, a whole series of trials; again and again, from the assembly of the doctors at Poitiers in the spring of 1429, through the long trial at Rouen and the Rehabilitation proceedings twenty years later, to the canonization process dragging through half a century, solemn gatherings of ecclesiastics have met to pass judgment upon her; and she is still on trial. She still divides opinion especially French opinion, as she did in her lifetime; she still is called devil and saint, and she remains, in the twentieth century, a factor in contemporary politics and war.

In 1429, when Joan so suddenly moved to the forefront of the historical stage, France was in a state of utter devastation and distraction; the Hundred Years' War with England had been in progress, with intervals of quiet, for almost a century, and it had been conducted entirely on French soil. It was, in reality, that most destructive and terrible form of war, a civil war. England, the smaller, less wealthy and populous of the two countries, was able to wage aggressive war against France only because of that country's internal divisions, and in particular because of the power and self-assertiveness, vis-à-vis the Crown, of the feudal princes.

In 1429 the national cause centered on the dauphin Charles who was supported by the interest of the Duke of Orléans and who held most of France south of the Loire; his followers were called Armagnacs, after the county of Armagnac in the south of France. Leading the opposition to him was the powerful Duke of Burgundy, Philip the Good, who controlled most of the north and east of France, including the rich cloth towns and trading centers of the Low Countries, and who was yoked in a somewhat uneasy alliance with the English foeman of his *soi-disant* liege lord, the dauphin Charles, who claimed the style and title of king.

All Gaul, then, was divided into the two parts, Armagnac and Burgundian; and the reaction to Joan of Arc's meteoric career was divided strictly upon these party lines. To Armagnacs generally, she was a saint of God, sent to bring about the coronation of the lawful heir to the throne in the cathedral at Reims. Burgundians were equally sure that she was the child of the Devil—a witch, or at best a brazen impostor, doing the Devil's work by aiding the vicious and cruel Armagnacs. As for Charles, they looked upon him as a worthless fellow, bastard son of an infamous mother, Isabella of Bavaria, conceived during one of the worst fits of insanity of his mad "father," King Charles VI, and having, therefore, no true hereditary title to the throne he sought to seize.

In view of this state of opinion, it is not surprising to find that contemporary French chroniclers of Joan's career (the sources upon which all later accounts of her are based) fall as sharply into two camps as did contemporary opinion generally. Joan moves through the chronicles of her own party surrounded from the beginning by a kind of nimbus of miraculous happenings, like the cloud of white butterflies which some thought they saw fluttering about her standard. In the Burgundian accounts, on the other hand, this nimbus becomes a sinister penumbra of suggestion about witchcraft.

The student who approaches these documents for the first time cannot but be immediately struck by their confusions and contradictions. Almost every detail of an event so much discussed in them as the siege of Orléans, for instance, is beset with dispute and controversy; in despair, one is tempted to conclude that history, so far from being an exact

science, is indeed, as Voltaire called it, *une fable convenue.*

Even when friendly, the chroniclers often give scant details of Joan's life; to them, she is only one of the actors in a great drama. They were often paid chroniclers, one of them attached to every great baron, as in the case of Perceval de Cagny, cited below; so we find one Tringant saying that his master did not spend any money in order to obtain mention in the chronicles and thus was omitted from them.

It would seem that these materials, as dubious as they are copious, must be used with the greatest caution. If we did not have the trial and had only these, Joan of Arc would be indeed a vague, half-legendary figure. It is true that even a liar may speak the truth now and then, but it hard to know when he does so.

The chronicles of the Armagnac party, from the period 1430–70 (all, needless to say, favorable to the Maid), are, after the record of the trial and Rehabilitation, the sources chiefly relied upon by modern historians. The earliest of these chroniclers is apparently Perceval de Cagny, whose work was brought to light by Jules Quicherat, the greatest of the Joan of Arc scholars. Quicherat never wrote a biography of Joan, but expressed his views on the more controversial points in 1850 after he had completed a careful editing of the sources in his huge five-volume *Procès de condamnation et de réhabilitation de Jeanne d'Arc* (1841–49). His views were heavily influenced by De Cagny, whom he found terse but exact; and, as almost all the innumerable biographers of Joan in the late nineteenth century and since have followed Quicherat rather slavishly, the influence of De Cagny upon them has been tremendous.

Perceval de Cagny was master of the horse to the Duke of Alençon, one of the powerful princes of the blood royal of France who was married to the daughter of the Duke of Orléans, the poet-duke who had been a captive in England since Agincourt. As Alençon's relationship with Joan was a close one, De Cagny is most favorable to the Maid. He was with the Alençon family forty-six years, and it would appear that he kept a journal. He does not know much about the Maid save when Alencon was involved. He was present at the coronation campaign of Charles VII, but after the autumn of 1429, when Alençon and Joan were separated, his chronicle becomes hearsay. His central theme is that the Maid performed miracles and would have done more had she not been thwarted by the cowardice, sloth, weakness, stupidity, and jealousy of the King and his council.

A consideration of Alençon's later history will discount the heroic Sir Galahad image of him and will show him in his true, fully formed character, as a typically insubordinate, rebellious, adventurous feudal noble, turbulent, jealous, violent and fiery, contemptuous in his attitude toward the King, useful to the royal and national cause only if kept under firm control. He seems to have dabbled in witchcraft and was rather credulous, vain, and flighty. He lived to be tried twice for treason and to be charged with seeking "powders to dry up the King." In 1440 Alençon, Joan's "beau duc," was one of the leaders of the fierce feudal revolt against Charles VII, called the *Praguerie,* in which self-seeking nobles waged ardent war against the Crown at a time when the struggle with England was still going on. In short, his later record does not incline us to accept his estimates of affairs at court, nor those of his henchman, Perceval de Cagny. Perhaps the best that can be said for this chronicle is that, whatever its weaknesses, those of the other Armagnac chronicles are even more glaring. All of them belong to hagiography more than to history.

Modern French historians usually feel a patriotic contempt for the Burgundian chroniclers as being traitors in league with the national enemy—"fifth columnists" as we should say today—and so, though essential to a rounded view, they are seldom cited. Most English and American writing, influenced by French models, has likewise adhered closely to the Armagnac tradition, clerical, conservative or monarchist, nationalist or romantic. Yet, though they find few defenders in the court of current public opinion, the Burgundian chroniclers include a number of the most important fifteenth-century historiographers. Some of them have a sceptical, cynical realism that seems curiously "modern" in tone. The Burgundian tradition contains inaccuracies, no doubt, and leaves a great deal unexplained, but it

may also contain truths which the orthodox version neglects.

The Burgundians, of course, did not regard themselves as traitors. Charles VII, aside from his doubtful legitimacy, had been barred from the succession for complicity in the foul murder of Jean sans Peur, Duke of Burgundy. By the Treaty of Troyes, Charles's own parents, King Charles VI and his queen, Isabella of Bavaria, had repudiated the claim of their son, and this repudiation had been ratified by the *parlement* and by the estates of the realm.

The Maid's visions, so exalted in the eyes of the Armagnacs, become "foolish phantomries" or imposture in the eyes of the Burgundians. They point out that her prophecies were not always fulfilled and sometimes grievously misled her followers. They usually recognize Joan's courage, and her influence on the course of events, but they tend to see it as something fearful, monstrous, unnatural. Her conduct seems to them vicious and immoral, vain and cruel, and she herself a lowborn pretender to divine inspiration—a detestable woman, the laughingstock of her sex, the scandal of men.

For example, Monstrelet, the chief Burgundian chronicler, has scant appetite for Joan's miracles and cannot accept her undeniable equestrian skill as a miraculous endowment. The Burgundians and the English had generally circulated the story that she had learned to ride as a chamber-wench at the inn at Neufchâteau, and that she had lost her virginity there. Joan herself admitted at her trial that "for dread of the Burgundians" she stayed "about a fortnight" at the inn at Neufchâteau and at that time assisted its proprietress, a woman named La Rousse. Doubtless the episode was thought to be a humiliating one, minimizing the heroine's social status in a society where such matters were all-important, affording ground for the propaganda of the enemy, and casting doubt upon her virginity. We may dismiss that doubt, for even her trial judges, who had verified her virginal status by causing her to be examined physically by the Duchess of Bedford and her ladies, did not dare to question it, though to have done so would have been much to their advantage in proving her guilt, since there was a prevalent belief that the Devil could not make a pact with a virgin. Joan was

undoubtedly virginal; but she may have stayed at the inn longer than she admitted at the trial.

Despite the general assumption of historians that Joan's words are infallible, there is really no reason whatever to assume that she told her judges the truth, the whole truth, and nothing but the truth. She herself cautiously said to them that there was a saying among little children, "Men are sometimes hanged for telling the truth." When first exhorted to take oath to speak the truth, she answered, "Perhaps you might ask such things that I would not tell." Finally, she swore to tell the truth "concerning matters of faith." Next day, after swearing the same oath, very reluctantly, she said to Beaupère: "You may ask me such things, that to some I shall answer truly, to others I shall not." Ultimately, she swore "to speak the truth of what I know concerning the trial," a sufficiently limited and ambiguous undertaking! Similar altercations occurred at later sessions when it was sought to put her on oath. All this is not much more reassuring to the observant historian than it was to the judges. The whole effect, moreover, of Joan's answers at the trial would suggest that they are full of *suppressio veri* and hardly deserve the implicit faith that has very generally been placed in them. We can understand why the eminent doctor of the Sorbonne Jean Beaupère, testified, even amid the general whitewash of the Rehabilitation, that she was subtle, with all the subtlety peculiar to women.

The career of Joan of Arc has traditionally been regarded by historians as the turning point in the Hundred Years' War. It has also been assumed that her execution was one of those crimes which are worse than crimes, since they are also blunders; that it left the sainted Maid a martyr, enshrined in popular memory and more potent in death even than she had been in her lifetime. But this is far from the case. Following her death she was almost forgotten, especially by the great and powerful even of her own party. The news of her fate was received in a kind of stunned silence, succeeded by oblivion. In 1433, at Blois, Jean Jouvenel des Ursins, in an assembly of the three estates of the realm celebrating the glories of the reign of Charles VII, marvels that

For the relief of Orléans, Joan was given 4,000 men and a citizen army under Dunois, the Bastard of Orléans. The city was only lightly held by the English, and victory was easy. Nevertheless, the battle was a tonic to the French. It was followed by a string of minor successes, culminating in a marvelous victory at Patay (opposite, as shown in the Vigils*), where the French lost three men to 3,000 for the English. This seemingly miraculous event, as well as the liberation of Orléans, was widely set down to the Maid's divinity.*

"a small number of valiant heroes to whom God had given courage to undertake the cause sufficed for such an enterprise," but he says not a word of the Maid. She had become, apparently, a compromising circumstance in the life of Charles VII, to be forgotten as soon as conveniently possible; doubts concerning her mission had deepened into negative certitudes by the trial at Rouen.

We must remember that the tribunal which condemned Joan was a tremendously impressive array of the leading ecclesiastical talents and reputations of the time—almost a synod of the Church. One need not, therefore, be surprised that the verdict of such a tribunal dealt Joan's reputation a shattering blow. The trial at Rouen was commenced very deliberately and with great publicity; and yet, even seven months after the plan for trial had been announced, there was no public intervention from Charles VII, from the Archbishop of Reims, or from Rome.

The outcome of the Rouen trial was certainly pleasing to the English, yet the idea of a Church trial of Joan originated, not with the English, but with the University of Paris. It seems difficult, despite the almost universal execration to which Joan's judges have been subjected in modern times, to read the trial record without feeling the deep sincerity of the ecclesiastics in their quarrel with Joan—their shock, for instance, at her male dress! The University was sincerely Burgundian and Anglophile in sympathy, of course, and it pursued Joan with conviction. It stood behind the tribunal which tried her, and which (despite later attempts at evasion on the part of several of its members) found her to be a heretic, a sorceress, schismatic, and apostate. However unintelligible these sentiments may be to modern French patriots, there can be little doubt of their sincerity and good faith, and equally little of their immense moral authority throughout Christendom; for the University of Paris was then at the very height of its immense medieval fame and influence as a theological authority.

It is clear, therefore, that in the two decades following Joan's death it appeared that her name had been branded, presumably forever, throughout Christendom, in a sentence which did not appear to be English, but Gallican and Cath-

olic. The Vice-Inquisitor, Jean le Maistre, was a timid and feeble individual, but his signature upon the chief legal instruments of the trial was invaluable throughout all Europe, for it directly implicated the papal power. To say he had done wrong would be to "undermine all human authority."

In the last analysis, however, the mainspring of the whole procedure was that redoubtable personage, Pierre Cauchon, Bishop of Beauvais. No one, in his time or later, could challenge Cauchon's claim to great ability, or to thorough legal and theological training; he was one of the brightest lights of the University of Paris. His letters, inserted at the beginning of the record of the trial proceedings, reveal him to be an able man of business and of large affairs—precise, direct, authoritative. He was no brute; he showed both humanity and good judgment in opposing the use of legally permissible torture upon Joan, upon the ground that it was "neither necessary nor expedient." It is one of the ironies of history that this man should have gone down, alike in popular and in literary tradition, as one of the blackest villains of all recorded time, worthy of comparison only with Pontius Pilate, because of his leading part in the trial of a peasant maid from Lorraine whom, we must believe, he regarded sincerely as a heretic and a witch. Nothing could illustrate better than the fate of Cauchon's reputation, the fickleness of fortune and popular favor, the vanity of human ambition. But, in any case, we must recall Cauchon's weight and repute in the eyes of his contemporaries in order to understand clearly the prestige of the trial he conducted, its legal rigor, and its great impact upon his time.

And yet, in spite of her disgrace, there exists a good deal of evidence that Joan was not completely forgotten. The upper classes, many of whom in her lifetime had viewed her claims with jealousy, scepticism, suspicion, or fear, were glad to forget her; but the common people, who had acclaimed her in life, did not forget her so readily. They felt instinctively that she was one of them, sent for their succor and consolation. Marvelous stories of her exploits continued to circulate.

It is in the atmosphere thus created that we have the strange and rather mysterious episode of the "false Joan of Arc"—or "false Joans of Arc," for we cannot be quite sure

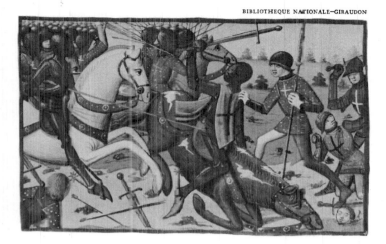

now whether there were one or several pretenders. The careers of those martial Maids showed that Joan's popular cult, which had so flourished during her lifetime, was already growing; her achievement had been sufficient to assure that men would not quite let her die; perhaps it showed, also, that some of the influential and official personages who had found her useful during life still found her memory useful and her successors convenient. The career of the "false Joan" was in a way a kind of anticipation of the Rehabilitation, except that it did not have the sanction of the Church—was, in fact, very far from having such sanction.

Men, we may conjecture, did not quite believe in the "false Joan"; they merely wanted to believe in her. This must be the explanation of the fact that in Orléans, where Joan was so well known, men feted Jeanne des Armoises, the pretender, and at the same time continued to say masses for the repose of the soul of Joan of Arc. Joan's mother never acknowledged any would-be impersonator of her daughter; it is curious that Joan's brothers did so, but no doubt they found the "false Joan" a useful connection, a useful ally in their military and official careers. After all, were they to challenge someone who must have had powerful and authoritative support?

Charles VII, however, did not abandon forever the goal of "rehabilitating" Joan of Arc formally and officially; on the contrary, he pursued that goal with characteristic tenacity. Charles pushed through the Rehabilitation on the ground that the judgment of Cauchon dishonored him, despite the fact that the original trial is, regarding him, a "masterpiece of reserve." What shame in the future if enemies could declare that a king of France had retained a heretical woman, and one in communication with demons, in the ranks of his army! Charles VII wished to crown his victory by removing the slur which his enemies had cast upon his triumphant coronation in the cathedral at Reims. It is not without reason that Shaw, in his play, has the King say: Provided they can no longer say that I was crowned by a witch and a heretic I shall not fuss about how the trick has been done.

The Rehabilitation is marked by an earnest search for formal legal defects in the trial. To break a sentence *pour vice de forme* was a favorite medieval device. It is, of course, a moot point whether the defects of form detected in Joan's trial are real or largely imaginary, as thought the great scholar Quicherat, who wrote a masterly analysis of the trial and Rehabilitation.

It would be remarkable indeed if a man of Cauchon's intelligence and legal training had allowed his *beau procès* to be marred by the kind of obvious legal flaw which the Rehabilitation attempted to find. No medieval heresy trial, one may be sure, could have stood up under such a raking as was given this one.

It is hard not to be impressed by the cogency of the evidence which Quicherat presents for the view that the trial of Joan of Arc was indeed *un beau procès*, conducted by a great lawyer and sound in canon law, regardless of the Rehabilitation's strictures. This view in no way passes a verdict on the trial from the point of view of ideal justice, as conceived in a later age; a legal system, of course, reflects the reigning ideals of its own age. Perhaps the truth is that man's concepts of justice were changing in the fifteenth century, and the Rehabilitation is really a condemnation of the old inquisitorial order in the light of new and more humane ideals of justice which were coming into being. There is no doubt of the ability, learning, and sincerity of the Rehabilitation judges, as there is, to our mind, little doubt of the ability and sincerity of the original trial judges whom the Rehabilitation so much maligned. The human mind is easily self-deceived. It seems reasonably clear to us that in response to royal and popular pressure, the Rehabilitation judges convinced themselves that Cauchon and his associates were grievously at fault alike in character and in method. In other words, Cauchon and the other judges were the scapegoats for the institution which they served, and have remained so ever since. We can trace a parallel "will to believe" in human devils and personal scapegoats even in our own time—in war-crimes trials, for instance.

The condemnation of Joan's original judges in part took the form, however, of finding legal flaws in Joan's trial under the old rules, even where those legal flaws did not exist.

In that way, a direct challenge to the old order was avoided and a necessary tribute was paid to the innate conservatism of mankind. All history shows that men accept new things most readily when they present themselves in traditional guise. All the great revolutions, Protestant, English, French, American, even Russian, go back to some lost excellence.

The Rehabilitation was conducted in such a manner as to minimize the opening of old sores, the reawakening of old controversies. There was no general indictment of those who conducted Joan's trial; a number of them, in fact, testified at the Rehabilitation and showed as much zeal in 1456 as they had in 1431. Only certain scapegoats were selected, and those safely dead, beyond the reach of judicial recrimination.

Pierre Cauchon, Bishop of Beauvais, was dead, as were most of the judges; the Promoter, Jean d'Estivet, a personage of the second rank, was also deceased; and the Vice-Inquisitor, Jean le Maistre, could not be found. These men were saddled with the whole responsibility for the assumed miscarriage of justice in the case of Joan of Arc; and influential living ecclesiastics, such as Courcelles, were thus protected. Nobody appeared to defend the accused judges. Nobody, therefore, had any reason to fear or hinder the commission of inquiry; in fact, quite the contrary. Joan's judges and assessors had been unanimous in their verdict; but the Rehabilitation record contains evidence of sympathy and support for Joan which is not at all apparent in the original trial record. No doubt time, and changing political circumstances, mellowed the memories of Joan's judges. One judge even denied participation in Joan's trial although his name figured in its *procès-verbaux* and in the registers of the indemnities paid to the judges!

The Pope, Calixtus III, apparently would have liked to protect that devout servitor of the Church, Pierre Cauchon, from infamy. Representing him as having been duped by the false reports of D'Estivet, he called him a bishop of good memory. It proved impossible, however, to rehabilitate Joan while at the same time salvaging the reputation of Cauchon. He appears in the Rehabilitation proceedings as an inhuman brute, with an aspect in utter contrast to that which he bore in his lifetime. When Warwick says, "The King is ill-served, since Joan has escaped us," Cauchon's reply, as alleged, is, "Be of good cheer we shall catch her yet." Joan's second judgment was really the judgment of her judges.

In general, the Rehabilitation proceedings are very sparing of miracles, and more than one theological quagmire is deftly skirted. No doubt the judges did not wish to ask of the Pope any more than they could help, fearing reluctance and opposition; they made the minimum claim upon a pontiff in an Italy in which Renaissance scepticism was already at high tide. Some of the wonderful stories which enshroud Joan's memory had not yet had time to form.

The Rehabilitation record is, of course, the source of the touching and beautiful stories of Joan's edifying end, on a pyre so elevated that death must come slowly. We learn of the tears of her judges, of those, at least, who could bear to witness the spectacle. We hear of John Tressart, secretary to the king of England, who exclaimed, "We are lost; we have burnt a saint!" We are informed of the word "Jesus" in letters of flame at the burning, and of the white dove which flew away from the flames toward France; it was seen by the English soldier who came to add a fagot to the pile but who fell on his knees when he heard the cry "Jesus" from the midst of the flames. We hear of the executioner who feared that the fact that Joan's heart was not consumed meant that his victim was a saint. We are told of Joan's final affirmation that her "Voices" had not deceived her. We learn that she died embracing a cross, her eyes fixed upon another cross held before her by a sympathetic priest.

We are spared here the horrid realism of the Burgundian chronicler, the "Bourgeois of Paris," who tells us that after the burning the ashes were pushed aside to expose the body so that all might see that it was indeed that of a woman; and no doubt, also, so that all might see that the witch of the Armagnacs had not escaped by aid of the Devil, or of wicked and abandoned men.

In sum, what is the value of the Rehabilitation as historical evidence? That its value is considerable can be doubted by no one. If it is used with care, every part of Joan's career is illuminated by it. The real problems arise as to the trial record and the Rehabilitation. Which are

we to follow, where the two differ? Here we find a wide spectrum-band of opinion among scholars, to whom both records have been freely accessible. In general, the more a writer approaches the clerical school of opinion, the more he accepts the Rehabilitation completely and gives it priority as evidence, using it as a touchstone to test other sources. The more closely, on the other hand, a writer approaches to the agnostic or rationalist position, the more he treats the Rehabilitation with reserve and scepticism, tending rather to use the trial record as a touchstone. In short, his attitude to the Rehabilitation and to the trial is likely to furnish us with a master key to any writer's general philosophy, as well as to his attitude toward Joan of Arc in particular. From his view of the Rehabilitation flows his interpretation of the Maid.

Since the Rehabilitation of Joan of Arc, completed in 1456, more than five centuries have passed. We cannot here attempt to achieve more than a bird's-eye view of the vicissitudes of her reputation during this great period of time. In portrait and ballad and mystery play, the fifteenth century presents us with a folk-heroine; the view of her is sometimes primitive, often artlessly imaginative and fanciful. In François Villon's simple and profoundly moving allusion to her, we have the comment of high art:

> Et Jehanne la bonne Lorraine
> Qu'Englois brulerent a Rouan;
> Ou sont ilz, ou, Vierge souvraine?
> Mais ou sont les neiges d'antan?

Joan of Arc the virago, the strumpet, the heretic and witch, perhaps a puppet, perhaps an impostor—this is the Joan of Arc of the French Renaissance, of the earlier English tradition, of Shakespeare in *Henry VI, Part One*, and, at least in some aspects, of Voltaire and Hume and other less eminent thinkers of the eighteenth-century Enlightenment. The memory of the "false Pucelle" is one ingredient in this image of the *egregia bellatrix*, which, in Renaissance courtly literature, displaces the folk-heroine of the fifteenth century.

Joan of Arc was not of great interest to the Renaissance humanists of that century and the next. She was, indeed,

"too Gothic" for their tastes; too plebeian in origin, we may conjecture, for an era of aristocratic culture; too nationalist for an age still, in large part, cosmopolitan in its cultural ideals. No great statues were dedicated to the Maid in this period, no great dramas were written about her. She is assimilated, however, in tapestry and in Latin epic, to the tradition of the Biblical and classical heroines; she is Deborah, she is Jael, she is Judith, she is Esther; she is the Sibyl of France; she is Cassandra, she is Velleda, she is Semiramis; she is Camilla, or Hippolyta or Penthesilea, queens of the Amazons; or, she is Bellona, goddess of war. Her sacrifice rivals that of Iphigenia. She has the courage of Clelia, perhaps the virtue of Lucretia. She is even compared to Hector or Achilles or Hercules! Her virginity, however, is sometimes questioned, her supernatural inspirations generally ignored, her military and political judgment often denied, directly or by implication.

The Protestants of the sixteenth century saw Joan of Arc as the Joan of the Rehabilitation "tainted with idolatry," identified with Church and King. They destroyed every representation of her upon which they could lay their hands. Swedes in the service of France who ravaged Lorraine, even cut down the fairy tree near Domrémy, *l'arbre charmine faée de Bourlemont*, which was prominently mentioned at Joan's trial.

Later generations of Protestants, however, have often adopted quite other attitudes. Some of them have accepted as valid the original view of Joan, arrived at by the Church court that tried her and condemned her to death; the view, namely, that she was a heretic. As such, she has been regarded by some Protestants as a forerunner of the later Protestant movement.

To the *philosophes* of the Enlightenment Joan was, at best, a skillfully dressed *machine de guerre;* at worst, something of a fraud. Of course, the writers of the eighteenth century did not have the documents before them, so it was the easier to minimize the Maid's qualities of mind and will, which showed themselves so clearly in her trial. Joan stood identified with the Church which had rehabilitated her, and the monarchy which she had so stoutly championed; and

she shared in the disfavor of these two increasingly unpopular institutions in an age which was notably deficient in historical imagination and saw the Middle Ages as an era of dismal gloom. George Bernard Shaw's Joan, a precursor of nationalism, could have but little meaning to the cosmopolitan and often rather pro-English thinkers of the French Enlightenment. In fact, she made more appeal to the Scottish philosopher, David Hume, who, in his *History of England,* reflecting the humanitarian outlook of the age, condemns her treatment by Bedford as "barbarous and dishonourable":

This admirable heroine to whom the more generous superstition of the ancients would have erected altars, was, on pretence of heresy and magic, delivered over alive to the flames, and expiated by that dreadful punishment, the signal services which she had rendered to her prince and to her native country.

The French Revolution was a decisive event in the development of the reputation of Joan of Arc, as it was in the development of everything else in France. In its immediate effect, it was a further blow to her reputation, already badly battered by the assaults of the Enlightenment on the eve of the Revolution. Whatever "pasts," real or fictitious, or half one, half the other, were being resurrected by the various partisans, the Gothic age was not one of them; no revolutionary party looked back to it. The thinkers of the preceding century, who had traduced the Maid, now reigned in their glory; and when Voltaire's mortal remains were borne in a triumphal car to a resting place in the Panthéon, it was not to be expected that his overwhelmingly unfavorable verdict on the *Pucelle* would be widely discounted. Later Republicans might see in her "the revolutionary gunneress and captain of the National Guard," in Anatole France's phrase; but this conception was not the dominant verdict of the great Revolution itself, though it was not an idea completely unfamiliar at the time. In the main, the Revolution viewed Joan with hostility, seeing in her the prop of Church and King, the beatifically smiling heroine of the Rehabilitation. Her relics and her monuments were swept away; though her devoted city of Orléans insisted on naming after her one of the cannon cast from her bronze image.

The way was therefore open for reviving conservatism to appropriate Joan unchallenged, and to make of her one of its icons. It is not surprising then, that under Napoleon I, when many of the discarded ideas and institutions of the old regime began to reappear in a new and rather unstable synthesis with the creations of the Revolution, Joan of Arc came back into fashion. Napoleon aimed at national unity against the English, and she was surely its appropriate symbol. The First Consul sought to detach her from her ties with the *ancien régime* and to convert her into a support of the new and more splendid throne which he planned. He could find a use for the "Gothic" Joan of Arc and for her religious associations. His official reconciliation with her was proclaimed by him in the *Moniteur,* the official gazette. The decree restored the annual Orléans fete on May 8, the anniversary of the raising of the English army's siege of the city in 1429, owing largely or entirely to Joan's intervention. Soon after the restoration of the fete, a new monument to Joan was erected with the approval of Napoleon. This new monument, a ridiculous work and a travesty upon its subject, faithfully reflected the artificiality of the attempted Joan of Arc revival, as well as the atmosphere of military emergency which had largely inspired it.

The nineteenth century has been called, by a German writer, "the century of the *Pucelle.*" It was inevitable that the restored monarchy after 1815 should find Joan of Arc useful. Before the Revolution the French monarchy had sustained Joan's reputation because she had been instrumental in the crowning of the King. After 1815, however, it was rather the other way about; it was Joan who sustained the reputation of the French monarchy. The monarchy had few claims to military glory, at least in more recent times; and it had to compete with the military achievements of the French Revolution and Empire. The martial exploits of Joan were, therefore, important as a source of military distinction, traditionally linked, as they were, with the monarchy.

Joan was, moreover, not only associated with the King and with the Church, which after 1815 was a main support of the King; she also had ties with the aristocracy, since she had been ennobled by Charles VII. Above all, she was a patriotic and popular figure, peasant-born; although in the Restoration period there were not lacking those who tried to show that she was really of noble or even of royal descent —perhaps a bastard princess. Her remarkable career seemed, perhaps, to require an equally remarkable explanation. In the main, however, the French Revolution had made her peasant origin and her patriotic creed great assets to her reputation, which flourished accordingly. A spate of books, learned and popular, appeared in which she was dressed out quite literally in the elaborate habiliments, the plumes and furbelows, of a great lady of the Restoration. Her home in Domrémy and other places associated with her for the first time became objects of pilgrimage and popular interest. In the twentieth century French monarchist literature assumes increasingly a proto-fascist form, but in this form it continues to find Joan of Arc useful. She, who was burned as a heretic, becomes, ironically, the heroine of the Right.

Another movement which after 1815 contributed no less than did monarchism to the growing interest in the Maid of France was the romantic movement. There were many reasons why the romantics should have been interested in Joan of Arc. She was to them the child of nature, the daughter of the people. Believers in salvation through scenery projected her against the background of her native fields and forests. It was in this light that she was seen by English romantics such as Southey, De Quincey, and Landor, no less than by the great German romantic Schiller or a French romantic such as Alphonse de Lamartine. Michelet gave a romantic historian's interpretation of Joan in some of the most celebrated pages of his *Histoire de France*. Verdi and Tchaikovsky presented Joan as she appeared to the romantic musician. A famous passage in Tchaikovsky's opera gives us her farewell to her native woodlands, *Adieu, Forêts;* in this, Tchaikovsky follows Schiller closely. Conservative opinion, after Chateaubriand, "took up" the romantic movement and gave it a Gothic turn; romantic painters presented Joan against a Gothic background. Such sculptors as Dubois, Frémiet, and Anna Hyatt Huntington also exploited this theme; others, such as Chapu and Rude, continued the trend of the earlier romanticism in presenting Joan as a peasant maid.

Many and complex are the uses of Joan as a symbol of French nationalism in the nineteenth century. French nationalists debated with the Germans over the possession of Joan, for some German writers claimed that since she had been born in Lorraine, then part of the Holy Roman Empire, she was not really French at all. Natives of Champagne and other French patriots maintained that she was really born in that province and that, therefore, as a "Champenoise," she was indisputably French.

It is easy to understand how Joan, as a Lorrainer, became after 1870 emblematic of those lost provinces, Alsace and (in part) Lorraine, which many Frenchmen wished to redeem from the national enemy. In her pride and in her suffering, Joan was the very symbol of a bruised and suffering but invincible France which "stared hypnotized at the gap in the Vosges." The spirited monuments erected at this time in Nancy and even on the Ballon d'Alsace were symbols of this Irredentist sympathy. In the eighties there begins an arduous and pertinacious struggle, finally successful, to make the anniversary of Joan's triumph a *fête nationale*. She continues in our own time to be a rallying point for French nationalism of all types. André Dahl's novel *Jeanne d'Arc Revint* even pictures Joan's return for the purpose of chasing the Americans from Paris!

In general, we find that Joan of Arc all over the world is to many people a symbol of nationalism. We find her presented in this light in the national literatures of peoples as remote from France as Latvia and Poland and Brazil. In Maltese there are books which present Joan as a nationalist symbol. There have been Jewish theories of Joan of Arc, which have, explicitly or implicitly, identified with Joan the Jewish people, suffering and persecuted through the centuries; Joan thus appears again, in yet another role, as champion of the downtrodden. It is interesting to contrast the "Celtic theory," which, inspired by chauvinistic nationalism, suggests absurdly enough that Cauchon was a Jew and makes Joan a symbol of opposition to Jews!

American biographies, plays, histories, dealing with Joan

of Arc were, in the nineteenth century, usually echoes of their European counterparts. In the work of Mark Twain, however, we may catch an authentic reflection of the rough, brawling exaggerations of frontier humor and of the sentimental frontier attitude toward women, who have, in a new country, a scarcity value! Joan of Arc, too, was a favorite with pioneer American feminists like Sarah Moore Grimké. To Fentonville, writing in Richmond as the shadows of defeat closed about the Confederacy, Joan was the embodiment and the inspiration of a national *guerre à outrance*. Albert Bigelow Paine produced a more sober version of the sentimentalism of his friend Mark Twain, whose biographer he was. Francis Lowell, a judicial-minded Bostonian, provided, however, in his *Joan of Arc* what we must esteem the most solid historical work upon the subject of the life of the Maid in our language.

In the period of World War I, Joan of Arc was to Americans the sentimentalized symbol of the Franco-American alliance and of the cause of the *Entente Cordiale*. Popular ballads, bric-a-brac, medals, art exhibitions, alike expressed this sentiment; so did the noble monument, the work of Anna Hyatt Huntington, which stands on Riverside Drive in New York City. W. P. Yancy's *Soldier Virgin* catches the mood of the period. In Holman Day's *Joan of Arc of the North Woods,* and in the popular songs *Joan of Arkansas* and Jerome Kern's *Joan of Arc Was On Her Own When She Was Quite a Child,* we hear a raw and raucous note distinctly North American.

Following World War II there has again been a revival of the Joan of Arc cult in the United States, appearing even in women's clothes and in advertisements of the most varied sorts. The revival, this time, has had little to do with Franco-American relations. Perhaps there is something somewhat synthetic about this new phase of the perennial interest in Joan of Arc; it has centered about Maxwell Anderson's rather shoddy play *Joan of Lorraine,* which had a good run in New York with Ingrid Bergman in the leading part; and it has centered, also, about the expensive but rather unsuccessful film which was inspired by the Anderson play, and which also offered the Swedish actress as the Maid.

The fortunes of Joan's reputation have in recent times been much affected by the policy of the Roman Catholic Church. The *"fille de Dieu,"* as we have seen, played her part in the Catholic revival which accompanied the Restoration in France. The Neo-Catholicism of the period following 1848 further elevated Joan's reputation, and the number of works appearing which were devoted to her steadily increased. Finally, in 1869, the celebrated cleric Mgr. Dupanloup, Bishop of Orléans, the city which was always the center of the "Joan cult," launched the movement for Joan's canonization. The defeat of 1870, weakening the position of France very greatly, may have delayed the canonization; it would appear that a party at Rome, backed undoubtedly by German and other influences of the Triple Alliance, long delayed action of Joan's cause, which, however, moved deliberately through its various stages. Meanwhile, in France, Joan was the focus of a tremendous outpouring of scholarship designed to support the cause of canonization.

France, with her allies, was victorious in World War I, and she emerged for the time as the dominant power on the Continent, linked to the Church in new compromises by the fear of Bolshevism and by the problem of Alsace-Lorraine, in the main a devoutly Catholic region and now returned to France. The victory of France was echoed in the final triumph of Saint Joan, admitted in 1920 to the full glory of sainthood, at once national and universal, in stately ceremonial at St. Peter's. Since the *fête nationale* in her honor was also established, she was now, in every sense, the Saint of France.

In the course of the nineteenth and twentieth centuries, various new sciences have contributed new views of Joan of Arc. Modern scientific historiography was first to the fore in this difficult field. The labors of many scholars, of whom perhaps the most notable was J. E. J. Quicherat, brought to light the buried "sources" and placed them in print, duly edited and annotated. Every step of Joan's career was made the subject of varied and multitudinous researches. There were translations of leading source materials, such as the trial and Rehabilitation, into French and English. In the

works of Francis Lowell and Andrew Lang the scholarship of the Anglo-Saxon world made its contribution; and a number of leading German scholars, of whom Prutz was perhaps the foremost, also contributed notably; but all these multitudinous labors have brought little diminution of the controversy about the Maid.

The psychologists, too, had something to say about Joan of Arc from the standpoint of their fast-growing science. Various theories of hysteria and objectification, of schizophrenia and paranoia, were advanced. Anthropologist Dr. Margaret Murray's work on the witch-cult, with which she has sought to link the Maid, reminds us of those modern necromancers, the spiritualists, who have not been slow to claim her and to make much of her reported feats of clairvoyance, clairaudience, and prophecy. At the same time, the spiritualists carry on the tradition of antagonism toward the Church on the part of her old enemy, the wizard. Léon Denis, in a work translated into English by the celebrated spiritualist Sir Arthur Conan Doyle, has well stated the contention of this school of thought:

A constant stream of inspiration flows down from the invisible world upon mankind. There are intimate ties between the living and the dead. All souls are united by invisible threads, and rhythm of the universal life. So it was with our heroine.

The great loss of life in the First World War gave such views an increased currency; men and women turned to the occult for a species of pseudo-scientific consolation through the alleged achievement of communion with the dead.

Modern art movements too contributed new and often startling interpretations of the Joan of Arc theme. Realism, impressionism, post-impressionism, cubism, surrealism—all of these have commented upon her. The painting of Touchagues, the sculpture of Barrias, the modernist music of Honegger, and the expressionist drama of Georg Kaiser—each of these presents Joan in a new and somewhat strange light. But it is, above all, Jean Anouilh's *The Lark* that has achieved a brilliant triumph of experimental technique in the drama.

In our own day, in the mighty crisis of World War II, the "Joan legend" has undergone a new and startling development. The Vichy regime in France, continuing the long-

established tactic of French reaction, sought to use Joan of Arc as a weapon against Britain and against the cause of democracy. Some of the most effective posters of Vichy recalled to the French that the wicked British burned Joan of Arc and exiled Napoleon to Saint Helena. She was used by the Pétainists in an attempt to discredit altogether the British alliance and any dependence on the perfidious Anglo-Saxon powers. On the other hand, General de Gaulle and other patriotic leaders saw in Saint Joan of Arc the protagonist of their own crusade, which fought for the liberation of France from the foreigner. Gaullist Catholic writers, such as Jacques Maritain and Georges Bernanos, turned to Joan with an especial eagerness as the appropriate emblem of the nation's struggle for freedom, and it was in consequence that the Cross of Lorraine, from the coat of arms of Joan's own province, became the symbol of the Gaullist movement for national independence and for the restoration of the territorial integrity of France, from which Alsace-Lorraine had again been wrested. Each side in the great struggle, in other words, sought to appropriate the story of Joan of Arc as its own weapon. World War II closed, therefore, with Joan of Arc established in a new and a more exalted sense as the patron saint of France. In contemporary France the tradition of the Maid is securely identified with the *mystique* of General Charles de Gaulle, the Liberator who now, as President of the Fifth Republic, rules and leads the France which he seeks to regenerate and restore to her former glory.

Whatever future vicissitudes France may undergo, we may be sure that Joan of Arc will have a part in them and that her reputation though it may undergo new metamorphoses, will always, in France, be secure. For all time, Joan is France. The world at large, too, will admire her heroism as long as heroic courage is respected. It is in order to accord her the reverence which is her due that each age has had to reshape her in accordance with its own ideal. She belongs to universal history, in the sense in which Lord Acton used that phrase when he said: "By universal history I understand that which is distinct from the history of all countries, and is not a burden on the memory but an illumination of the soul."

By WILLIAM K. ZINSSER

A LITTLE FLIGHT MUSIC

Good morning, ladies and gentlemen. This is Captain Smathers welcoming you aboard your Peerless Airlines DC-80 Jetfloater flight 902 to Los Angeles. Our movie today will be the adult Biblical epic "The Passionate Legions," in CineMagic X80, starring Charlton Lancaster and Sophia Lollobrigida and featuring Walter Brennan as the emperor Diocletian. Your air hostess, Miss Smiley, will start the movie as soon as the aircraft is aloft and the "No Smoking" sign is off. We estimate that the picture will run four hours and eleven minutes, with an intermission after the burning of Antioch, at which time we will land at Omaha for refueling and popcorn. Passengers disembarking at Omaha may ask Miss Smiley for a synopsis of the remainder of the film, or write directly to Epic Pictures, Aviation Division, Hollywood 33. We expect to be cruising at an altitude of 18,000 feet, but the cabin is pressurized starting at three feet, so you should experience no discomfort. Our air speed will be approximately 300 miles per hour, and our ground speed will be 200 miles per hour. This discrepancy, caused by the fact that the earth is round and the air is flat, is fully explained in the informative booklet *You and Your Flight!*, which will be found in the pocket directly ahead of you, next to the airsickness bag, which you may want to use during the scene when ten Christian martyrs are mangled by tigers in the arena at Smyrna. This scene should begin shortly after we cross the Mississippi River at Moline and will conclude ten minutes after Cedar Rapids. I will be pointing out to you certain interesting sights along the way. Meanwhile, Miss Smiley and the rest of your Jetfloater crew join me in hoping that you enjoy the movie. We'll be taking off in just a minute now, as soon as we get clearance from the tower. There are only twenty-three planes stacked up over the field waiting to land, and right after that we'll be off. By the way, that roaring you hear under the left wing is nothing to worry about. We had a little trouble with the automatic de-sludgifier a while ago, and that noise is simply the cleaning compound doing its job. . . . Good morning, ladies and gentlemen, this is your air hostess, Miss Smiley. I'm sorry we were so long in getting clearance. You may unfasten your seat belts now and stop observing the "No Smoking" sign. In a minute Miss Mirth and I will serve you cocktails and start the movie projector. If there is anything that you do not understand about the movie, please do not hesitate to ask us. Simply press the button next to the reading light except on seats 9, 17, 24, 36, 48, 59, 71, 86, and 101, which are the emergency escape doors. Kindly do not leave by these doors while the movie is in progress. . . . *Oh, Smartacus, thank God you've come! The Roman columns are marching toward Byblos at this very moment. What chance has a poor slave girl like me got against such Barbarian swine? . . . Never fear, my pretty little Flolita. Take these two thousand piasters and run to Damascus over the Baalbek road. Go to a man called Paul in a street called straight and tell him I will join you there as soon as the moon comes over Mountolive. Tell him . . .* Hello again, ladies and gentlemen, this is Captain Smathers. If the screen is a bit wiggly, we're encountering a little weather, but we should be out of it in another twenty minutes—I hope in time for the boiling oil scene. That girl, by

the way, is Sophia Lollobrigida. You'll see when the screen is clearer. . . . *Say, you're a tasty little dish of figs, aren't you? What's a looker like you doing all alone on the road to Damascus? Notice how easily my fingers press into your pretty white flesh. . . . Leave me be, you heathen beast! When Smartacus hears about this he'll squash you like the foul insect you are! . . . Aha! I've been trying to trap Smartacus for three long years. With you as bait he's sure to* . . . Ladies and gentlemen, Federal regulations require that when flying over land we demonstrate this life preserver, which you will find under your seat. As you see, it is easy to operate. Simply pull the red toggle knob downward with a sharp thrust, like this, and if it fails to open simply tug the green counterloop sideways with a revolving motion, like this, which activates the flare dispatcher, the flashlight, the whistle, and the zipper. One precaution: do not effectuate these steps while you are still inside the aircraft as that will markedly hamper your escape. Thank you. . . . *But Paul, how can we warn Smartacus in time? . . . Tut, tut, my child, you must have faith. Was it not said in Galilee that the wicked would fall like wheat? Besides, I knew a certain pharmacist in Aleppo who* . . . Say, folks, in just a minute you're going to get a dandy view of Sandusky, Ohio, out the left window. We don't often see it as clear. Sandusky is known for its jute mills and crampon factories. You can just see them beyond that bend in Route 37A off to the left. . . . *Begging your pardon, Emperor, but why should we worry about a little handful of religious nuts? . . . You're young, my boy. Maybe when you get a little older you'll see that faith can be a mighty*

potent weapon. . . . All I know, Emperor, is if you'll give me a hundred men and ten lions I'll clean those religiosos out fast. That's what your Uncle Caligula would have done. . . . Hmmm, perhaps it's worth a try. . . . Ladies and gentlemen, we've just heard that Omaha is closed in. They're having a bit of weather down there. Hurricane Zula; got up from Shreveport faster than anyone expected. We're going to put back to Bermuda, but don't worry, we won't interrupt the movie; and if it ends before we get down, we've got another movie aboard —Jerry Waldo's super-adult drama for adults only, "We Were Adulterers". . . *But Paul, how did you know the Emperor's lions wouldn't harm us? It was a miracle like how they turned on Diocletian's mercenaries instead. . . . My child, things happen that man in his vanity can never fathom. How can I make you understand? Perhaps if I recall an event that took place long ago beside a date palm in Jerusalem. I was sitting* . . . Ladies and gentlemen, this is Miss Smiley. During this flashback, which isn't very interesting, Miss Mirth and I are going to serve you your Jetfloater dinner, prepared for your eating pleasure in our Jetfloater kitchens in Pocatello Falls, Idaho. Miss Mirth and I regret that we cannot serve you your dinner and keep the movie in focus at the same time, especially during the electrical storm that we are about to pass through. But as soon as your Jetfloater dinner is over we will pick up with the siege of Ephesus, which was filmed with a cast of thousands on location outside Ephesus, Illinois, with the full co-operation of the Illinois government. Now, please fasten your seat belts again. We do hope you are enjoying your movie and your flight.

THE NEVER REPRESSIBLE BEECHAM

By NEVILLE CARDUS

By the time he died last year at eighty-two, the imperious conductor had said and done so many outrageous things around the world as to provide his obituary writers with columns of witty and wicked anecdote. But the legend of Sir Thomas continues to grow. One of his best friends and severest critics, Neville Cardus, long the music commentator of the Manchester Guardian, *here adds fresh substance to Beechamiana in an intimate portrait of the waggish maverick who was also, amid his fondness for heaving dead cats into sanctuaries, a first-rate musician.*

My first meeting with Sir Thomas Beecham was at the Salzburg Festival in 1931. I was astounded one day in the Festival's second week to get a telephone message from Sir Thomas asking me to lunch with him at the Europa Hotel. Although we had exchanged some correspondence before this year, I didn't dream that he wanted to know me personally, and so with some trepidation I went to the Europa.

To my unease and, at the moment, my disappointment, we were joined in the dining room by Lady Cunard, birdlike and voluble (and a formidable patron of the arts). Sir Thomas introduced me as "of the Manchester *Guardian.*"

"Ah," quick-fired Lady Cunard, "ah, now, Mr. Cardus—you must write an article—protesting against this English obsession of foreign music—we can do just as well in England—so please, write at once a strong article in the Liverpool *Post.*" "Manchester *Guardian,*" prompted Sir Thomas.

"Ah, yes," prattled Lady Cunard, "you know it is simply absurd—the adulation in England of all that is foreign—really, Mr. Cardus—please write a very strong article in the Yorkshire *Daily Post.*" "Manchester *Guardian,*" insisted Sir Thomas, chewing his short Imperial.

"Ah, yes," persisted Lady Cunard, taking new breath, "it is too ridiculous —this blind worship of everything foreign in music—you simply must, Mr. Cardus, make a strong protest in . . ."

"The Manchester *Guardian,*" prompted Sir Thomas yet again, this time his voice a little weary. I found myself in a new world of comedy and play in which conversation was a game, a "situation," to be savored histrionically. Sir .Thomas's entire waking days and years were presented to an audience: he was a comedian. Or, as this is a term which the English associate with red-nosed buffoonery, I had better describe him as an artist in comedy. But he was not a wit in the epigrammatic way of Oscar Wilde, with whose retorts Beecham's are often compared.

Sir Thomas indulged not so much in wit as in waggery. He was not eighteenth century of manner in the least: he belonged entirely to the nineteenth century. For all his poise of behavior, his deliberately fastidious voice and vocabulary, he remained at bottom a Lancashire man. The suave accent, his button boots (in those days), his measured diction, didn't deceive those of us who knew him well. With Sir Thomas blood was thicker than Pol Roger. Away from the concert platform he never hurried, not even while crossing a busy street. One morning after a rehearsal of *The Messiah* in the Queen's Hall a day or two before Christmas, we were about to go into the Langham Hotel for lunch. I produced from my pocket a new Dunhill pipe and said, "I know it is impossible to give any sort of Christmas present to you, Sir Thomas. But here you are—and, please try not to forget all about this one." He took the pipe, thanked me, and, with a split second of hesitation, sang to a Handelian cadence, "It shall be smoke-*ed.*"

Where did he come from? A Lancashire family enriched by the manufacture of pills. His father, I am told, spoke un-

inhibited Lancashire speech. But though some Lancastrian gusto, even some hint of provincial arrogance, might break out in moments that found him off guard of his poise—a poise made second nature by long, conscious practice—Sir Thomas's image to the public had no suspicion of regional characteristics. On the contrary, he exhibited himself as the entirely sophisticated man of the world.

At times I suspected that he erected

a façade to hide from the world an uncertain Beecham, a Beecham afflicted with a feeling of inferiority, of some frustration in himself. He would admit no shortcoming in his mental and musical equipment. I never heard him express disappointment with his own share in a concert or opera performance. Occasionally his conducting was as slapdash as well could be; to such a level of unconscious bluff on the rostrum could he descend that often I have blushed for him. Several times I chastised him in print and by word of mouth after he had roared and rattled the orchestra through a composition. Invariably he would reply, "Like most of your fraternity you are from time to time visited by tone deafness. The performance in question was one of my very finest. . . . You might like to know that only this morning So-and-So rang me up to tell me he had never heard a better." So-and-So might be anybody from Richard Strauss to his own first trombone.

He housed no demon that preyed on and devoured his creative, or rather his re-creative, tissue of nerves, sensibility, and power of musical thinking. He was not the haunted, tormented artist, ever deploring that his reach went far beyond his grasp. He was, in a word, vain—in two words, intractably vain. He would go into a fury at any deprecation of his activities, on or off the platform, mental or physical.

In all the countless hours I spent with him, nobody else present, I rarely heard him refer to religion. To women he referred once, saying that none was worth the loss of a night's sleep. His reading was extensive rather than wide. He did nothing to correct or modify personal prejudice. He was allergic to anything German. "How can you read Goethe?" he would ask. "He was a colossal and conceited bore, and something of a dabbler." (He by the way, knew little German.) Heine, of course, appealed to him, good translation or bad. "He was a Jew, therefore not even the German language could get in the way of his wit." German music he pretended to belittle; but at the bottom of his heart, he respected it. Bach was one of his pet aversions. "Too much counterpoint—moreover, Protestant counterpoint." "And Wagner. . . ?" "A genius, no doubt; but too often excessively theatrical and emotional. Lohengrin was his only stylish work—the Germans have no idea of style." "But what about Die Meistersinger?" The fugue in the overture, he said, was the crudest example in existence of that always dreary form of music. But on the whole he admitted the broad humanity of Die Meistersinger, adding that whenever he conducted this opera he needed for the time being to forget Mozart's Figaro and the Falstaff of Verdi. He delighted in French lyric opera: "I would give the whole of Bach's Brandenburg concertos for Massenet's Manon and would think I had vastly profited by the exchange. Bach composed in only two tempi—quick and slow. Bach's music is associated in Protestant countries with Biblical texts, which are sacrosanct. Nearly all the questionable works of the great musical geniuses have been prompted by religion, or by implications of religion. For instance, Wagner's Parsifal, the Requiem of Brahms, and Elgar's Gerontius, described by my friend George Moore as holy water in a German beer barrel. . . . Dvorak's Stabat Mater, Gounod's Redemption—what dreadful crimes have been committed in the name of religion! Gounod normally was a sensitive artist, and Dvorak composed an enchanting symphony—the Fourth. The Missa Solemnis is mostly second-rate Beethoven, or rather, it is third-rate Beethoven. The best of Beethoven's music, excepting the first four of his piano concertos, and the Third, Fourth, and Sixth symphonies, are second-rate, measured by values set up by Mozart. . . . Vaughan Williams? I very much like his Fantasia on a Theme by Tallis. Unfortunately, in his compositions published subsequently he omitted to take the precaution of including a theme by Tallis."

Sir Thomas took delight in maltreating a composition he didn't like. On one occasion he found himself obliged to conduct the "Pastoral" Symphony of Vaughan Williams. Moreover he was audacious enough to rehearse the symphony without score. He just "followed" the players. The symphony ends with an orchestral descent to near silence, then a soprano sings the final cadence. Sir Thomas, after waiting until the voice died away, waiting with a superb show of impatience, turned to the first violins and made an imperious downbeat. No instrumentalist, of course, produced a sound. "Why don't you play?" asked Sir Thomas. Quite a number of people were present at this rehearsal, so the first violin, wishing to save Sir Thomas's face, whispered, "There's nothing else to play, Sir Thomas." "Nothing else to play?" queried Sir Thomas in a loud, unashamed voice, audible throughout the hall. "Thank God!"

Sometime in the 1930's he astonished me by telling me that he proposed to present Alban Berg's Wozzeck at Covent Garden, which was then under his direction. "I shall go into the country, and study the score." Three or four weeks later I received an invitation from him to lunch at Abbey Lodge, his address (of many addresses) at this time. When the valet led me to Sir Thomas's room, the strains of "Un bel dì" from Madame Butterfly floated on the air. And as I went into his room Sir Thomas was at the piano. "Why Puccini?" I asked. "I am trying to wash Wozzeck from my mind and memory," he said. He did not present the music-drama at Covent Garden, needless to say. "It is an ingenious score," he admitted, "but entirely uncivilized and uncharming. I am not interested in music, or in any work of art, that fails to stimulate enjoyment in life, and, what is more, pride in life."

Yet he was not really a narrow-minded reactionary. When he was fairly young in years, he introduced London, and nearly all the important cities of England, to music that was at the time called "modern"—Stravinsky, Delius, Debussy, Ravel, and the Russians. He even conducted the A-flat symphony of Elgar. Beecham severely cut this work and Elgar protested. At Sir Thomas's next rehearsal of the symphony he addressed the orchestra thus: "Gentlemen, the composer of this immortal masterpiece objects to my abbreviations. So now we'll play it as written—with all the repeats." The point of this ironic arrow will be felt by musicians who know that the A-flat symphony is governed by an endlessly recurring "motto-theme."

He accepted an invitation in 1928 to conduct the New York Philharmonic. This magnificent orchestra was then in the charge of Toscanini, who at the time was far away in Italy. Beecham was called in as a temporary substitute. After his first rehearsal with the New York players, he was taken to lunch by the orchestra's committee—large, opulent men crinkling with dollar notes and aromatic with enormous cigars. They asked Sir Thomas to give his opinion of the Philharmonic. "They are quite incredibly good," he said, flavoring his Havana; "their technical command is abnormal. . . . I have rehearsed Rimsky-Korsakov's *Scheherazade* this morning. The woodwinds and horns executed the most difficult arabesques like Kreisler on his violin. Really wonderful." Now the menacing pause. "But for all this dexterity of techniques, I found the players extraordinarily insensitive interpretatively. No idea of an alluring phrase." Another pause, then—"Tell me, who has been conducting your orchestra lately?"

Like many men sharp of tongue, he was—as I have already suggested—extremely sensitive to criticism of himself He withdrew my press tickets for the whole of a Covent Garden season because I had taken him to task for putting on *Der Rosenkavalier* with unintelligent cuts. In drawing attention in the Manchester *Guardian* to Sir Thomas's scissoring of the opera, I was fully aware that it is often produced with excisions. My point was that Sir Thomas's cuts in Act One were not fair to the Baron Ochs, and that because of them the audience would be left wondering why the Marschallin so heartily despised him in her outburst, "Da geht er hin." Sir Thomas picked up his pen and rushed into print, defending himself by attack. He wrote a letter, not to my paper but to the *Daily Telegraph*. His point was that in the second week of December, 1912 (the performance occasioning my criticism was about 1934), he had gone to Berlin and discussed the production of *Rosenkavalier* with Strauss and his publisher. "On no occasion," wrote Sir Thomas, "was the suggestion ever made that the work should be given in its entirety." But I had written to Strauss in Garmisch about the matter, and the composer assured me he had not consented to the cuts, adding that he had "to put up with them so long as the inviolability of works of art were not protected by law."

Like most of his colleagues, Sir Thomas was seldom impressed favorably by any exponent of the mysterious art of conducting except himself. After a slapdash concert on the pier at Bournemouth, when he seemed determined to drive the Fifth symphony of Beethoven into the sea, he entertained a number of friends in his suite. During this midnight repast the conversation got on the subject of conductors. "Toscanini?" asked Sir Thomas. "What do I think of Toscanini? A glorified Italian bandmaster! Have you ever heard the lively band competitions in Paris? Toscanini would have found his métier there."

A pretty girl nervously put forward the name of Bruno Walter. "Bruno Walter? Malodorous, my dear. As for Koussevitzky, I doubt if he can read a score at all. Richter was a mere time-beater. I admit that I was very young when I heard him, but my earliest impressions of his conducting were confirmed by Cosima Wagner. Weingartner no doubt had a very fine musical culture. But he became slower and slower. We possess conductors of our own who are the equals of, not to say the superiors of, any of these foreigners." (In later years he asked why we in England engaged at our concerts so many third-rate Continental conductors, since we had so many second-raters of our own.) He had a good word to say of Furtwaengler, whom he invited to conduct *Tristan und Isolde* at Covent Garden. But when I stated in my notice of the performance that Furtwaengler's interpretation of the opera was the best heard in London in many long years, Sir Thomas withdrew my tickets. He himself had conducted *Tristan* at the Garden.

Until he approached that venerable period of life during which the British people take even an artist unto their bosoms unquestionably and unconditionally, Sir Thomas was not exactly a popular figure. "Why doesn't he pay his income tax?" the British people asked, not knowing the complications of his financial position. "Why doesn't he live with Lady Beecham?" (his first wife). At about this time he walked to the conductor's desk at a concert in Birmingham in complete silence. He bowed to the audience. Not a handclap, not a sound. Whereupon he turned to the orchestra. "Let us pray," he said.

Sir Thomas has told us in his autobiography, *A Mingled Chime*, how he came by the reputation of being bankrupt. I cannot here go into the extreme complexity of it all. But in time Sir Thomas emerged from this financial labyrinth more or less successfully. Like his old friend Ernest Newman, he had an acute and well-informed brain for figures. Nonetheless he gave his accountant, one of the cleverest in London, many a headache. One morning the latter spoke to Sir Thomas by telephone. "Sir Thomas," he said, "I've been going into your affairs until the crack of dawn, and now I'd like you to enlighten me on a most crucial point—do you owe, or are you owed, two million pounds?" "The answer is in the affirmative," replied Sir Thomas, "in both cases."

It was in Australia in 1940 that I first got to know Sir Thomas well. This was his only visit to Australia, and he took possession at once. In his Sydney hotel he had waiters, page boys, and the manager himself running around like lackeys. The director of music of the Australian Broadcasting Corporation invited him to give an interview over the radio with myself as the interviewer. I asked Sir Thomas to rehearse with me. He had not talked on the air before; nevertheless he declined to rehearse. "I prefer in these matters to improvise. Just you say a word or two, put any question you like to me, to start me off. After all, my dear fellow, listeners will want to hear me, not you." So we went on the air without script, without preparation at all.

I began by asking: "Now, Sir Thomas, you are about to conduct orchestras entirely strange to you. Tell me, do you agree with the old saying that there are no good or bad professional orchestras, only good and bad conductors?" I breathed with relief; I could, I imagined, now sit back and be entertained, in common with all listening Australia, by half an hour of Sir Thomas. The fact is that for once in his lifetime he dried up. After a half a minute's silence—an eternity in time measured by radio—he snapped back at me: "What precisely do you mean?" Completely stunned, I repeated the question, adding by way of variation, "only good and bad conductors—I believe it was Von Bülow who said it." "Did he really?" responded Sir Thomas, skeptically, relapsing once more into sterile silence. Sweating heavily, I heaved the creaking wheel round again: "Do you intend to conduct much Mozart?" "Whether I shall conduct, to use your phrase, much Mozart, depends on the condition of the orchestras here—about which you have given me no information whatsoever."

Somehow we temporized through half an hour of disconnected dialogue. I remember that he told me—and at the same time told countless invisible listeners—that I was talking too much. "Listeners want to hear me—not you. Please don't interrupt." At the end of the broadcast, as we were leaving the studio, he took me by the arm in his most friendly, benevolent way and said, "There now—what did I tell you? All talks over the air should be impromptu—unrehearsed."

He, of course, told Australian audiences that they were ignorant, that he had seen more intelligent faces in the remote villages of Bulgaria. Students of the magnificent University of Perth, in Western Australia, reacted so touchily to Sir Thomas's diatribes that on the eve of his departure from Perth by sea, they boarded the ship and entered his cabin with the intention of cutting off his beard. But they found Sir Thomas asleep face down on his pillow.

In those years his manners at a symphony concert did not appeal to the taste of the "Establishment" of British music. My predecessor on the Manchester *Guardian*—Samuel Langford—took him to task on account of his acrobatic gestures as he conducted. At one concert his baton flew from his hand and nearly impaled the first trombone. Moreover, he was suspected of "amateurism"—long before Toscanini actually called him an "amateur." A complex character—Falstaff, Puck, and Malvolio all mixed up, each likely to

overwhelm the others. Rachmaninoff told a friend that he was unhappy about a forthcoming concert. "The conductor —So-and-So—he has no temperament. It is always so in England. Too many the English gentlemens." "But," his friend pointed out, "last year you said your concert with Sir Thomas Beecham was one of the best and happiest of your life." "Ah," rejoined Rachmaninoff, "but Sir Thomas is not one of your English gentlemens."

It was around 1931 that Beecham told me he was about to form a new orchestra in London. "But where," I asked, "do you hope to find the players? The BBC Symphony has taken the best." "Maybe," he admitted; "the BBC has indeed attracted the best known instrumentalists of Great Britain. But you'll see!" In 1932 the Royal Philharmonic Orchestra played for the first time at the Queen's Hall. The performance of the *Roman Carnival Overture* of Berlioz was staggeringly brilliant. But an otherwise highly finished performance of Mozart's "Prague" Symphony almost jerked me from my seat when Sir Thomas brought in the D-major principal theme, after the introduction, at the same adagio tempo instead of allegro. My notice next day called for some explanation of this curious treatment or maladjustment. In his flat in Hallam Street, while he was still in bed, working on a score, he took away my breath (not for the first or the last time) by assuring me that his tempo for the main theme after the introduction was authentic. "You are probably acquainted only with the published score . . . but I have seen the original manuscript written by Mozart's own hand. . . ." All the same, the next time he conducted the "Prague" Symphony the theme in question was "allegro" all right, and unmistakably.

Sir Thomas's capacity for deep feeling was not often or obviously hinted at in his studied deportment away from the concert platform or desk at the opera. He gave proof of it in my company only once, during one of the last evenings I spent with him alone, a few months after his second wife's sudden death. Speaking of her, he was obviously moved. "She was a wonderful comrade," he said.

"Comrade"—again the unexpected word. But for all his usually detached and "superior" manner, his vanities, and the impression he gave that even his closest friend was not essential to his way of life, is it a wonder that he was, especially in his old age, very much liked, in fact very much loved? The orchestras didn't call him "Tommy" for nothing. He did nothing by halves, whether in a good or bad, kindly or waspish mood.

On his eightieth birthday, at a lunch given in his honor in a London hotel, this is the way he finished his speech of thanks: "Years are nothing. Thought and feeling—notably feeling—are all that matter. Say what you want to say, with firmness and conviction. The one thing that is really important, in playing, in conducting—yes, and even in misconducting—is this: whatever you do, do it with conviction."

THEATRE

Where There is Total Involvement

I hesitate to open with a tautology, but the great fact about The Living Theatre is that it is alive. If Broadway is sick, as I am assured by all experts that it is, the malady may stem from excessive traffic in handsome corpses. However, the subject is not the morbidity of Broadway, but the vitality of an enterprise at Fourteenth Street and Sixth Avenue (up one narrow flight in a renovated neighborhood department store). Being alive, The Living Theatre is assertive, sometimes misguided, full of ego, insistent in its demands upon an audience, and given to making statements about itself. For it is a political theatre, and it exists, not to beguile, but to influence its audience.

Politics is the art of governing, and governing our understanding is the objective of Julian Beck and Judith Malina, founders, producers, directors, designers, and frequently actors in The Living Theatre repertory. Their most famous production, the play that has given the company a national and international reputation, is Jack Gelber's *The Connection*. It is notorious by now that nothing happens in *The Connection*. Indeed, its central point is that, in the world of narcotic addiction, nothing ever does happen; that the seduction of dope is its capacity to make events su-

perfluous. Verisimilitude is what holds attention at *The Connection,* an immediacy so tangible that only by a conscious appeal to common sense can one be assured that these are actors and not junkies. Therefore, if one thinks of the play in the context of entertainment, it becomes unseemly, a pandering to curiosity no more edifying than a tour of Chinatown. A good many people have thought of it in that way, but it is obtuse of them; the whole force of the writing and staging is to break down the distinction between actor and viewer and to make everyone present aware that, to a degree, he is hooked by an addictive society. That is political, as opposed to commercial or voyeur, theatre.

Since their purpose is to influence, the Becks (they are husband and wife) concern themselves a good deal with the enigmatic relationship of illusion and reality. "We believe in the theatre as a place of intense experience, half dream, half ritual, in which the spectator approaches something of a vision of self-understanding. . . . To achieve a full synthesis of experience, he must become totally involved, as in a dream or a religious ritual. It is in order to accomplish this that the avant-garde theatre today uses techniques developed by

Brecht, Piscator, Copeau, Meyerhold, Cocteau, etc." This statement, made by Mr. Beck in a New York *Times* article of several years ago, well defines the aims, methods, and preoccupations of his theatre. Over a period of ten years, he and his wife have drawn their repertory from Pirandello, Racine, Strindberg, Sophocles, Cocteau, Brecht, Gertrude Stein, Alfred Jarry, W. H. Auden, Paul Goodman. It is a literature, in the main, of poetry and legend directed to social and political ends; and it lends itself frequently to productions in which such terms as "stage" and "play" and "actor" become ambiguous, in which one cannot be certain where the line has been drawn between actuality and contrivance, or, indeed, exactly when the performance began or ended.

When the public arrives for William Carlos Williams's *Many Loves,* the curtain is open, scenery and props are being set, actors are working in groups upon details of the scenes to come. Gradually, more figures assemble, movement becomes livelier; then the lights black out momentarily (someone calls that a fuse has blown), and at this moment, presumably, the play begins. And during the intermission of *The Connection,* out in the spacious, elegantly impoverished lobby, where coffee and avant-garde publications are sold and where pacifist appeals are given out free, a member of the cast will panhandle you for money to finance his next injection. The Becks (between them they direct all the productions) look in the scripts for lines that can be flung like knives into the audience. Gelber once remarked, at a time when an English production of his play had provoked real riots at the Duke of York Theatre in London: "The conflict of attitudes between audience and players—rather than the conflict on stage—is the focal point." It is the recurring focal point in Living Theatre productions, and by concentrating on it, the Becks have found that they can operate, in a state of approximate solvency, the only true repertory theatre New York has known in many years.

Preoccupation with the mirror bafflements of illusion and reality stems in part from the political orientation of the company; it stems also from the Becks' involvement in the artistic currents of their era. Henry Miller writes autobiographies that are probably fiction; Jean Genet writes fiction that is almost certainly autobiography; John Cage composes music that is governed by chance; painters in every contemporary exhibition offer canvases whose subject is the paint on the canvas. The Museum of Modern Art has recently mounted a major show of "constructions"—works in which the objects of domestic and industrial life become the materials of art, and in which the materials tend to comprise their own subject matter.

It has become good form to explain this eating away of the distinction between creation and occurrence by referring to the world situation: reality has become so fantastic and so fateful that the artist recoils from tempting fate by the exercise of his own fantasy. But the breaking of forms can readily be elevated to the importance of a theory; it then becomes self-defeating, since it depends for its dramatic, poetic, or ethical effect on an expectation of the very forms it is transgressing. Shock is not a theory; it too soon becomes habit.

Because of *The Connection,* and because of their location on Fourteenth Street (the Boulevard Saint-Michel of the pad dweller), it is sometimes ignorantly said that the Becks are spokesmen for the hip and the beat. This suggests a dishevelment of demeanor and a modesty of ambition made ludicrous by the couple's elegance and boldness They have always been bold. Fifteen years ago, just out of college, they decided that the theatre was to be their life and that, in the absence of a company that attracted them, they would have to start one of their own. They started it in their own apartment (the enterprise was originally called The Living Room Theatre), which is modest enough; but they enlisted among their first sponsors and mentors Robert Edmond Jones and Jean Cocteau, and that was not modest at all.

Last year they were invited to participate in the annual Théâtre des Nations Festival in Paris and applied to the State Department's cultural exchange bureau for travel funds. Unhappily for them, money had been previously assigned to a Helen Hayes troupe that was also headed for Europe, and the cupboard was bare. The Becks may have suspected, too, that the State Department preferred Miss Hayes's unobjectionable repertory of *The Skin of Our Teeth, The Glass Menagerie,* and *The Miracle Worker* to The Living Theatre's package of controversy, *The Connection, Many Loves,* and Brecht's *In the Jungle of Cities.* By coincidence, the larger foundations also found themselves to be short of funds.

In this predicament the Becks staged a "champagne gala" at the studio of Larry Rivers, charging twenty-five dollars a couple and auctioning donated works by Franz Kline, Grace Hartigan, Willem de Kooning, Richard Lippold, Theodoros Stamos, I. Rice Pereira, and others. In an evening they raised more than half the money needed for what proved a triumphant barnstorming of Italy, France, and West Germany. The company won all three of the important awards at the Paris Festival.

As participants, then, in the contemporary sleight-of-illusion, the Becks share the hazards of the preoccupation. Having granted that they may take such liberties with theatre custom as advance their purpose, I yet wonder whether some of their more celebrated exploits really do advance it. Thus, the rather elaborate device of the play within the play of *The Connection*—the pretense that this is not a stage performance but the filming of a documentary and that the actors are really junkies who have been hired with dope to exhibit themselves before the cameras—is intended to make us feel we are "there." But in practice the cast on stage creates a mesmerically terrifying intimacy with the audience; whereas the periodic sallies of "director" and "author," down the aisle and up onto the stage, reassure everyone that the whole business is make-believe.

Similarly, the frame of "dress rehearsal" that surrounds the three very uneven sketches comprising Dr. Williams's *Many Loves* may interest those who have always wondered how one goes about staging a play. Possibly it was also thought that the spectacle of a young "playwright" trying to bring his vision to birth despite the blindness and jealousy of the "world" (his former homosexual lover, now a potential backer) gave sufficient point in Living Theatre terms to material that was not otherwise strikingly relevant. But the machinery only underscores the dramatic skimpiness of the author's reflections on love (though as quick sketches, two of the pieces are vivid and provocative), and the justifications in his alter ego's anxious monologues draw attention to the fact that there is reason for Dr. Williams's anxiety.

The Living Theatre is a small house (162 seats); the stage is elevated so little as to suggest that one might be looking from one room into another; there is no proscenium arch; there are no wings. More important, Julian Beck, who designs all the sets, has developed a style that, very close to the methods of "assemblage," seems to take canny

The Living Theatre lobby has two principal conversation centers, where actors often join the spectators between acts: around a bookstall-coffee stand (in the center) and below a frenzy of lead piping (at the rear), which ends in a drinking fountain.

ARNO STERNGLASS

advantage of discarded objects, scrap lumber, allusive mementoes, and decorations of the sort that clutter the attics of houses long lived in. His sets evoke precisely the atmosphere he intends; they satisfy the eye without unduly stimulating it (audiences, thank God, do not applaud Beck sets, as has become the stultifying custom uptown), and they efficiently support a clear, vigorous, and often complicated action in a tiny playing area. For all these reasons, then, communication flows with no hindrance between stage and spectator in this house. It does not need tricky machines to pump it.

Just how excellently it flows may be tested in the production of Brecht's *In the Jungle of Cities*, which Miss Malina introduced last season (it was the Amer-

ican première of a play Brecht wrote in 1921–1924) into the current repertory. The *Jungle* is a melodrama whose subject is easily stated—it is about a fight to the death between a Malayan lumber dealer and a poor boy from the country, in an imaginary Chicago of 1912—but it is almost impossible to know what is happening at any given moment. Having advised us in a preface to "judge without prejudice the fighting form of the contenders and keep your eye fixed on the outcome," Brecht proceeds to hurl so much dramatic debris at our heads that we should hardly keep our eye on an elephant, were one on stage. The play, permeated with nihilism, celebrates the decay of society at its urban centers, is contemptuous of aspiration and dubious of virtue. It is

written in a tone of high good humor by a young man who had respect for very few and very little, and who certainly did not include the audience in his select minority. You should find yourself ill-used by the play, defrauded perhaps; but Miss Malina so skillfully embraces cast and customers in the one human predicament that you feel caught up in a wry and universal vaudeville. Yet the production is marked by no newsworthy departures from theatrical deportment.

The Becks are right that participation is the key to life in the theatre. There must be an encounter, perhaps even a skirmish, between actors and audience. But I think The Living Theatre gets its skirmish most clearly when it reaches for it least elaborately. There is nothing new about living theatre: it was alive for the Greeks, it was alive for the Elizabethans, and it was alive for that mythical gold miner in Colorado who leapt from the stage box to save the heroine's flaxen head from the buzz saw.

However, it is clear from Jack Gelber's new play, *The Apple*, that The Living Theatre will continue at least for a time to scout the no man's land between illusion and reality. This play, the company's major work for the 1961–62 season, was originally announced for October and opened, after a series of delays, on December 7. The postponement of openings has become part of The Living Theatre's personality. The Becks do too much: they act in the current repertory, direct and design the new productions, plan the future; they promote the theatre on the air, raise money for an operation that is always a little in the red, support the causes that make demands on their consciences (I first talked to Miss Malina on a SANE picket line). On Monday nights, when there is no repertory performance, the house is host to concerts, movies, poetry readings, one-act-play series, lectures. The Becks also teach in The Living Theatre Studio, an important adjunct to the theatre. And next summer the company will again be abroad. It is too much—people can work as shock troops while a company is building, but this company has now been built. Pretty soon the Becks will have to stop answering every alarm bell.

In *The Apple* Mr. Gelber takes his preoccupation with the audience—his conviction that each member of it carries his own play on his back, like the addict's monkey—to the point where he has perhaps invented a new form, therapeutic theatre. On stage, the therapy is overt: a group of actors meets regularly in a Greenwich Village coffee shop (coffee is served by the cast from a counter on stage before the performance) to act out impromptu scenes that well up from their ids. These provide scope for a number of political and social jibes of varying sharpness and rather tenuous cohesion. *The Apple* is not acted ad lib, but

I suspect that much of it was written that way, and the top of Mr. Gelber's head is not infallible. On the evening in question, a paranoid (he is that chap who was making a nuisance of himself in the lobby before the show) erupts from the audience and injects himself into the playmaking. This results in a good deal of melodrama and further scrambling of fact and fancy, since the madman performs in earnest the fantasies the others conjure up within the bounds of their art. He also dies and is reanimated, with mystic results. The scenes jump rapidly from a replay of an old silent movie to a parody on the "good jungle doctor" to a domestic spat à la television to a moment of Old Southern decay. The actors move in and out of their roles like quick-change artists, and the only rule of association is that it must be free.

Despite the chaotic activity on stage, the cast finds time to maintain a running exhortation to the spectators that they drop whatever they are doing and "come over to our side." Since no one does—since indeed it is not literally intended that anyone should—the effect is a little like a Billy Graham rally at which not a single soul is saved. The theatre as a gymnasium for stretching the psyche may be a useful idea, but as conceived here it is a little too stridently frolicsome and not sufficiently developed. Gelber's play is wildly inventive, but that is not to say that it is consistently interesting. There is something a little half-baked about it—as when one of the girls announces that she would like to take on the whole audience by herself, a remark of the sort that produces titters in high school circles. One of the best actors in the troupe spends three-quarters of the evening pretending that he is a spastic. It was, he says, "an incredible opportunity for an actor," and that is precisely what I think it was not. Much too easy for a talented mimic. *The Apple* both sparkles and wavers; it ends up by asking a rhetorical question—isn't our stage more real than your life?—the answer to which is probably no.

But misgivings about *The Apple* do

not necessarily imply misgivings about The Living Theatre. The Becks run a house of experimentation, and by definition they will not always succeed. They are not selling packaged hits; they offer the excitement of work in progress and the satisfaction of a company that works from a consistent point of view toward a style that is both flexible and tough.

Repertory is the only situation in the theatre that nourishes style. The style developing at The Living Theatre is very close to that of the Becks themselves. Miss Malina displays a candor that is uncommon, if not unique, in this era of veiled intentions. It is a candor that disarms less than it challenges—even pacifists go armed in our world, and that is her weapon. Julian Beck looks like a Modigliani, and one feels he has pitched his resolve to a point of asceticism and then fleshed it with a quiet buffoonery. He is a very funny man, with whom one might hesitate to get funny. So the plays come at you from the stage with a shocking directness; they are cut lean and move efficiently to their conclusions (they don't always do so; I am talking of the vision and the successes). There is no "go for broke" hysteria in this theatre. A hit cannot make them rich (not with 162 seats and a $4.50 weekend top), and a flop cannot sink them. They are bound to fail from time to time because success is not what primarily interests them. But the chopping block does not operate here as it does on Broadway. *The Connection* opened in the middle of summer to terrible notices from the second-string critics; it was weeks before the periodical reviews, the belated cheers of the first-desk daily reviewers, and word-of-mouth enthusiasm attracted an audience. Uptown the show would have closed in a week, but the Becks carried it on the shoulders of their going repertory until it took on the main weight itself. At The Living Theatre no play fails until the Becks decide it has failed. That is repertory, the life in the theatre the Becks knew they wanted for themselves fifteen years ago. What goes on uptown is merely show business.   ROBERT HATCH

MOVIES

From Red Banners to Ballads

That marvelous social satirist Peter Sellers once did a savage and very topical dissection of a famous BBC program: the weekly gathering of critics who take up the latest film, novel, and painting exhibition. Sellers, playing the role of a moderator, asks in overripe accents, "Tell me, what do you think of the new Soviet film *Seven Brave Tractors,* now playing at Studio 9?" And the film critic replies: "I'm going to be quite frank— I *liked* it!"

This satire assumed, quite properly at the time, that all Soviet films could be characterized by the title *Seven Brave Tractors;* we have only to hear it and the dreary films of the later Stalin period begin to flicker in our memory: the stunning unreality of the young lovers, the *opera buffa* quality of life on the collective farm, the textbook-memorized patriotism. As a reflection of Soviet reality, they were about as valid as most Hollywood examinations of, say, life in the suburbs, or any of our current crop of TV "family comedies." Our amused superiority is of a piece, I think, with our pre-Sputnik notion that only American boys can take apart and put together an old Ford. When it comes to the production of non-art, we can match the Soviet Union, pound for pound, film foot for film foot.

There have been two other changes that date the Sellers routine. Soviet films no longer open at places called Studio 9 but at the most expensive art theatres in town (only Colombian coffee is served in the lounge); also, no critic need feel embattled if he admits to liking one of the films. Each showing is preceded by an announcement which suggests that the theatre owners and the film distributor are engaged in public service; the

imprimatur of the State Department's Cultural Exchange Program is presented; and we are assured that one of our films is at this very moment being seen by *them.* A woman behind me asked the question which was, I'm certain, in the minds of most of us: "Oh, God, I wonder what we're showing them?" *

Of the first nine films shown here as part of the exchange program, the most popular with American audiences have been *Ballad of a Soldier* and *The Cranes Are Flying;* and the critical response to *A Summer to Remember,* the latest of these films, suggests that it may prove to be the most popular of all. These pictures have one quality that gives them a tremendous edge over the Soviet films of the war period and the years immediately following: they are small. It is difficult to embrace an "epic," especially when it has quotes around it. However interesting to a cinema technician the Soviet war films may have been—the simulated battle scenes, for example, were phenomenal—the comic-strip heroics and the brazen and heavy-handed glorification of a tyrant caused them to be treated with contempt and indifference in the West.

Every film industry, as we know to our sorrow, goes through one or more periods of proving that it can make "big" films. The worst thing that has ever happened to the American film industry was not, as some maintain, the invention of sound but the invention of CinemaScope. That absurd elongated noodle of a screen has given film makers the means of indulging their worst tastes; they can now show Attila and ten thousand (count them!) Huns in the same frame, pillaging the entire civilized world. The manufacturers of sim-

* So far, the U. S. contributions to the exchange include: *The Rainmaker, War and Peace, Letter from an Unknown Woman, The Court Jester, The Adventures of Huckleberry Finn,* and *Little Boy Lost.*

ulated gold breastplates have been having a field day, and the voice coaches have been replaced with riding masters. The new Soviet film makers eschew the grandiose movie and its bloated effects; they have stepped back into the intimate world of the small screen with its handful of individuals and their relationships, which the camera can penetrate and explore so well.

The epic form in its real sense is more a part of the Russian tradition than of ours; and their retreat from it puts them in rather unfamiliar territory. Prince Mirsky, in what is surely the most urbane reference work ever written, the *History of Russian Literature,* insists on identifying "bigness" with importance. One cannot say he is wrong to call Tolstoy both big and important, but it does cause the reader some alarm when he all but dismisses Chekhov because of his smallness. Mirsky accuses us Westerners of having "reached a stage of mental senility" because we "can be satisfied only by the autumnal genius of Chekhov." In these new films East and West have, apparently, met at last—if only in senescence.

Autumnal is a perfect word for these Soviet films; they are gentle, nostalgic, and a little sad; the war is present, but it is its aftermath and the sense of loss among the survivors that concern the film makers. Nor is it any longer the bigness of war that is presented; there is, rather, an exploration of war in its smallness; the lost patrol tries to find a way through the German lines in *Cranes Are Flying;* and in the film *Ballad of a Soldier* the war is reduced to the story of one man.

Ballad of a Soldier begins the way most good ballads do, with the hero winning against impossible odds. There is an almost mythic quality about the opening scene: the hero engages in combat a German tank which chases him across a deserted, lunar landscape; gawky and frightened, he falls behind an antitank gun and, almost by accident, destroys the tank. For this action he is given a decoration and a furlough of a few days, just long enough to get home to visit his mother. On one train he helps a crippled comrade; on another he meets a pretty girl; he stops to deliver a message to the wife of one of his buddies and discovers that she is having an affair with another man. What sophistication this film has—and it has a great deal—lies in its very artful simplicity; anecdotal episodes succeed each other, and the director (with that look of knowing innocence that artists like to adopt) seems to be saying, "Look here, don't blame or praise me; all I'm doing is following this boy." Missing trains, hitching rides, he arrives at last at the collective farm, embraces his mother,

and returns to the front and (as in all ballads) his death.

Structured like a ballad and very consciously aiming at simplicity, the film is not concerned with a portrait in depth; the director devotes himself to recording some universal gestures of men and women in wartime, very much aware that viewers in all parts of the world will be able to understand it out of their own experience of war.

But after seeing several of these new films, one can conclude that the Russian simplicity is by no means limited to a cinematic ballad; it is in fact the basis of their new cinema. They have rejected what a follower of Tolstoy, denouncing certain nineteenth-century novelists, scathingly called "psychological eavesdropping." There is in these films the same puritanism of form that Tolstoy demanded of himself in his later years, and indeed demanded of all art. He condemned as "superfluous detail" the close examination of the human mind and analysis pushed to its limits.

"Grant me simplicity of style," is the prayer he wrote in his diary. Mosfilm Studios may very well by now have engraved this over its doors.

A Summer to Remember certainly might have been made by a studio which had taken this prayer for a slogan. It is about a six-year-old boy whose mother, a war widow, remarries. The child is at first suspicious and afraid of his new father but later comes to idolize him. By the end of the film his only fear is of being separated from his stepfather, who has been ordered to take charge of a collective farm hundreds of miles away. What we are seeing is the Soviet New Man in action. There is a remarkable beauty and innocence in the family relationships portrayed here. Watching it, I had the feeling that the makers of this film were congratulating themselves and their countrymen, were saying, "What a long way we have come!" I was reminded of Gorky, who wrote in his autobiography that his father was a very gentle man—he always removed

In a grandiose scene from Dovzhenko's Life in Bloom, *a typical Stalinoid propaganda "epic" of the late 1930's, Grigori Belov, as Michurin, the famed Russian botanist, acknowledges the flowers and the plaudits of grateful agricultural workers.*

By contrast Ballad of a Soldier, *starring Vladimir Ivashov and Shanna Prokhorenko, is an intimate, small-screen film in the new, romantic Russian style. Its propaganda, extolling Soviet patriotic and homely virtues, is far more subtle and effective.*

111

his boots before kicking his wife. Not only are the New Men better behaved, they are better provided; no special point is made of it, but the camera lingers over the toys, the well-dressed children, the new wrist watch. If this means little or nothing to us, it is certain to mean a great deal to millions in other parts of the world.

The technique of these films is seemingly casual, even downright careless; never do we feel the weight of a directorial hand. It would be a great mistake, I think, to believe that this is not precisely what is intended. We are in the presence of extremely clever film men who are determined to make us forget that we are watching a fiction, written by one man, directed by another, and filmed in a studio near Moscow. Even the film stock itself, grainy and gray, reminds us of newsreels rather than studios. We are meant to think of this as life itself: it is an exceedingly artful kind of naturalism, and on its own terms very successful indeed. The Soviet film makers have not given us any lessons in advanced film techniques; but I suspect we have a lot to learn from them when it comes to putting our best foot forward or to translating our ideas into cinematic terms comprehensible to the rest of the world. There is no doubt that these films are significant propaganda achievements.

The Cranes Are Flying, on the other hand, seems to have been made to prove either that Soviet film makers are not monolithic, or that they can do a Hollywood treatment as well as MGM—perhaps both. It is as glossy a war film as *The Best Years of Our Lives;* it reveals an absolute mastery of every cliché of Western cinematography. But within this slick framework (everything's up to date at Mosfilm!) the characters love and pine for each other and suffer the transports of Pushkin's heroes and heroines. There is a classic simplicity in the relationships; and the heroism is of that quiet and understated order which we are more likely to call aristocratic than communistic.

The simplicity of Russian movies, then, is the simplicity of art; that is to say, it is very cunning indeed. But I don't mean to suggest that there is anything sinister about this. Soviet film makers, like film men everywhere, are obviously seeking a cinematic means of reaching the greatest possible audience at home and abroad. By presenting representative men in universally understandable situations, they have come a long way toward achieving their aim.

WARREN MILLER

CHANNELS

The Creative Man at Work

One of the defining characteristics of the professional commentator is his complete independence of subject matter. For the exercise of his profession, he requires only someone who will listen to what he has to say, or who will print whatever he feels called upon to set down in writing. So supplied, he will comment until his listener departs or his space runs out. There are, it is true, commentators here and there who maintain that they will not comment except upon matters in which they are expert, but the limitation is more apparent than real; any commentator is capable of becoming an expert upon anything under the sun within the space of, say, twenty-five minutes, and most of us move a good bit faster than that. It is a competitive business—dogma-eat-dogma, as it were—and unless you get off the mark pretty quickly, the day soon arrives when a new commentator replaces you in the table of contents.

I am manifesting myself, you will notice, to be a professional commentator, and it is only fair that I present my credentials. I have been commenting upon other people's business for better than a quarter of a century. I began at the age of nineteen, when I was engaged to write a radio program called "The Marriage Clinic," doling out advice-to-the-lovelorn for fifteen minutes daily, five days a week. It is true that after six months I was fired; I had counseled a correspondent, over my rather extensive network, that he would be well advised to kick his wife humpbacked, and my employers decided this was rather heady stuff for a morning audience. I never did find out whether the man took my advice. In any case, whatever the consequences may have been for that particular marriage, my counsel left me commenting without portfolio for some months, until a newspaper succored me. Time has passed, and I have been commenting for pay or pleasure ever since.

I adduce all this because it emphasizes an extraordinary experience I had a few days back, when I came across an item upon which I am totally incapable of offering any comment whatsoever. I discovered it in an issue of *Advertising Age,* a magazine without which this column might well be impossible to prepare. The *trouvaille* of which I speak was uncovered in a recurrent feature (prudently anonymous) called "The Creative Man's Corner," in which current advertising is held up to scorn or, more rarely, admiration, in conformity with a set of criteria that I have never fully understood. I understand it even less, now.

"For Intelligent People," ran the headline on the feature, and there followed a reproduction of an advertisement for Chiffon Toilet Tissue. The advertisement, as reproduced, consisted of two innocuous pictures and ten words of text: "Just like a woman, Chiffon is both soft and strong." The Creative Man himself then embarked upon his analysis. He liked the advertisement. He liked it fine. That ad, he said firmly, has been "conceived by an intelligent creative person for the benefit of intelligent buyers." It was, he added, "a masterpiece."

Now, all of this I could comment upon, if I wanted to. It happens I don't want to, but I could. It is still another sentence from the same critique that has stilled my tongue and left my faculties numb. I will now quote it, in a paragraph all its own:

"It requires a considerable measure of creativity to think of comparing toilet tissue to a woman."

I have nothing to say. Not a damned thing.

This new brush with the Creative Man did stimulate me, however, to recall some remarks made not long ago by Charles H. Brower, president of Batten Barton Durstine & (I believe) Osborn. Mr. Brower must not be carelessly categorized by his august position at the helm of one of our more prestigious ad agencies. In the trade he is known to be something of a maverick. For example, from time to time he shows up at the office in a brown suit. And he lives in New Jersey. But despite these leftist tendencies, he has risen to the top of the heap and is a man to reckon with along Madison Avenue—a kind of radical Rosser Reeves.

Mr. Brower wishes to unleash the advertising industry and turn its aggregated talents to the task of "selling the United States to other nations." It is doubtful that any man could emerge as leader of BBD&O believing that such a suggestion is a novel one. The advertising in-

dustry has been begging to be unleashed ever since an advertising industry has existed. They never tell us who is leashing them, but they want to be unleashed. So we will credit Mr. Brower, not with a new notion, but with the restatement of an old one. There is nothing wrong with that.

I must remark in passing that Mr. Brower does not honestly hope to be unleashed. He expects, instead, that the machinations of Schlesinger, Galbraith, Bowles & Rusk, individually or in series, will prevail. Such as they, Mr. Brower states dourly, "are attempting to dismantle our only possible propaganda apparatus just when we need it most. It is much as though they had decided to disarm the U. S. Navy." I quote this statement because I don't entirely understand it, and therefore don't dare leave it out. It might be extremely trenchant. For one thing, it appears to intimate that Schlesinger is leashing the U. S. Navy, which I hadn't known.

The idea of involving the hucksters in foreign policy keeps coming up because it is so attractive, if you don't think about it. After consideration, however—about six minutes' worth—this air of relevancy disappears and the whole thing becomes frightening. Since a great many people habitually think about ideas for six minutes, and sometimes more, Mr. Brower's idea has never taken hold, and with any luck it never will.

By "selling the United States" I presume Mr. Brower intends to convey, somewhat elliptically, the notion of creating in the mind of the foreigner some kind of favorable abstract image of the United States—a corporate image, to use the jargon of his own dodge. At least I hope he means that. If he has in mind any notion of chipping away portions of Rhode Island and peddling them abroad, I object, on constitutional grounds. Mississippi might be another matter. But of course I really don't believe he means anything like that at all—he merely wants Germans and Koreans and Japanese and French to love us, the way we ourselves love A.T.&T.

Now, let us not underestimate the ad

industry. Mr. Brower and his fellows are canny hands at selling soap or cigarettes or breakfast food or even automobiles. But the ad industry, by and large, has not done an overwhelming job of selling corporate images. Look at their own. The industry is constantly moaning that nobody loves an ad man, not even another ad man. We might even offer a challenge to Mr. Brower: "sell" the ad industry to the United States, and we might let the ad industry try "selling" the United States to the heathen.

Meanwhile, I have no great desire to be represented abroad, in any fashion, by people who can (a) prepare the Chiffon ad and (b) be proud of it. And the worst of it is that, whether Mr. Brower knows it or not, in fact I *am*. The foreigner's view of the United States has been created in large part by the advertising industry, and by the mass media it has captured, like television, or very nearly captured, like the daily press.

The advertising industry is the force behind a monstrous mass of anti-intellectualism that inevitably seeps over our borders and comes to epitomize us abroad. Domestically, anti-intellectualism is bad enough. But you can live with a lot of it because the emotionalism and irrationality it promotes are homegrown, and come naturally. But you can't appeal to another country with your own private brands of emotionalism and irrationality, because they have their own brands, and the two don't jibe. If Mr. Brower wanted to unleash the ad men in an effort to convince most Americans that they ought to approach questions of foreign policy in some reasonable manner, and vote accordingly, that might help a great deal. But if people began to act reasonably, there wouldn't be nearly so large and thriving an ad industry, and I don't suppose Mr. Brower would want to do anything like that. Anyway, I am not sure he could.

We had better leave things the way they are. The Chiffon ad can't do anyone much harm. The Creative Man, as the Secretary of Propaganda, very well might. Sorry, Mr. Brower. Stay leashed.

STEPHEN WHITE

113

The Trail of the Splendid Gypsy

CONTINUED FROM PAGE 13

Kean was "sketch'd from life" by the cartoonist G. R. Cruikshank at the Theatre Royal, London, in March, 1814, when he appeared in one of the most popular roles in his repertory, Richard III.

suicide in 1792. His uncle, Moses Kean, who died in the same year, had been a ventriloquist-entertainer and the lover of Miss Tidswell.

Aunt Tid, as Kean grew to call her, was a sensible woman and a competent supporting actress who spent forty years on the London stage. She took care of Edmund for long periods when he was a child. She provided the framework of morality from which he often wandered and the basic view of his art from which he never swerved: a passion for emotional truth.

The facts about his childhood are relatively few. He was not only taught acting by Aunt Tid, he was trained as a pantomime Harlequin, a tumbler, a singer and dancer, and a bareback rider. It was an age that adored theatrical prodigies, and the boy made a number of appearances. Among them was a trip to Wales, where he gave a private performance of *Hamlet* for Lord Nelson and Lady Hamilton.

His adult career began when he was about fifteen years old where all acting careers began in those days, in the provinces. There were three first-class theatres in London: Drury Lane, Covent Garden, and the Haymarket. To appear at any other London playhouse was to get yourself blacklisted by the major theatres; and to get an engagement at one of the major theatres an actor had to prove himself in out-of-town theatres. Kean spent nine years in the provinces.

To some extent his physique must have worked against an earlier rise to fame. The public was used to "Roman" stars of noble presence, and Kean was short. (His autopsy report gave his height as 5 feet 6¾ inches.) His voice, although there are reams of testimony about its varying powers, was not a round, unblemished column of golden sound; it sometimes tended to hoarseness. His face, too, was more striking than conventionally handsome: lean, vulpine, with scowling brows and glittering dark eyes.

In addition, the style of acting he was developing must have worried some managers. It often moved audiences, but it was new and highly personal—not without poetry but much more "natural" (what we should call "realistic") than the current fashion. London was not eager for him.

The story of his nine years in the provinces is one of grinding work, poverty, disappointment, and humiliation. Explicitly the story proves his persistence, and implicitly it reveals the reasons for his growing alcoholism and other excesses. Today we can only marvel that the fire (and that is the operative word in Kean's life) was not extinguished by heartbreak and simple hunger.

One episode will illustrate. In 1811 he was left stranded in Ireland by a tight-fisted manager. He had by then married an actress named Mary Chambers, nine years his senior, and had two sons, Howard and an infant, Charles. They landed in Whitehaven, England, in July with a bundle of clothes and books, a dog, and not one penny. They decided to make their way to London, where Aunt Tid could at least shelter them until Kean could find a decent engagement. It took them five months to reach London.

They traveled, he and his wife and two small children, from village to town to village, in carts and wagons when they were given rides; eating as they could, not eating when they couldn't; sleeping in the worst beds of filthy inns when they could afford that luxury. (Even when they couldn't afford it, Kean drank.) When they arrived in a place where there seemed the slightest possibility of scratching up a few shillings, Kean would engage a hall, write out a few play-bills, and get the town crier to announce the show. He and Mary would perform scenes from various plays; he, *solus*, would do songs, dances, imitations. Thus they made their progress to London, where they arrived in December.

In the provincial theatres he played all kinds of parts— often danced and tumbled—hoping always for the London engagement that would establish his fortunes and give the opportunity to his quality. At last the chance came, but not before some further turns of the knife. Despondent of ever reaching the three best London theatres, in October, 1813, he accepted an engagement for the following January at the Olympic, a minor London house. On November 16, six weeks later, he received the long-desired offer from Drury Lane. Six days later, on November 22, his cherished son Howard died. Wrung with grief, Kean had to trot back and forth like a hopeful dog from Drury Lane to the Olympic, begging the Olympic to release him and Drury to be patient. The tangle was finally cleared; his Drury Lane debut was set for January 26, 1814, as Shylock.

Theatres operated differently in those days. Their closest modern parallels are opera houses. Every sizable theatre had a more or less permanent company and a standard repertory, and would engage a visiting actor for Shylock much as an opera house might engage a Rigoletto today. He would arrive a day or two ahead of time with his own costumes, go through a minimal rehearsal to establish outlines of movement, which varied little from theatre to theatre, and then would appear. A "directed" production, in our sense of the word, was virtually unknown; audiences went to see individual performances.

History is lucky as far as Kean's London debut is concerned. On that bleak winter night William Hazlitt, jewel among critics, was present. There were, he said later, about a hundred in the pit, for Drury's business had fallen off. (Kean's engagement was one of several desperate attempts to find an attractive new star.) Hazlitt wrote in the *Morning Chronicle* of January 27, 1814: "Mr. Kean (of whom report had spoken highly) last night made his appearance at Drury Lane Theatre in the character of Shylock. For voice, eye, action, and expression, no actor has come out for many years at all equal to him. The applause, from the first scene to the last, was general, loud, and uninterrupted. In-

"Out, out, thou wretch! Hence, leave me forever!"—Kean, again drawn by Cruikshank, appears as Barabas in Christopher Marlowe's The Jew of Malta. *The 1833 playbill announced Kean's first performance with his son Charles. It was also his last: he collapsed on stage during Act III and died several weeks later.*

deed, the very first scene in which he comes on with Bassanio and Antonio, showed the master in his art, and at once decided the opinion of his audience."

Kean knew it. He ran home to his lodgings after the performance and exclaimed: "Mary, you shall ride in your carriage, and Charley shall go to Eton!"

In many an actor's life the interest of the story would dwindle here. A struggle for recognition—but afterward just a straight, climbing line of success. The success certainly came. Through the years he essayed the great parts, one after another: Richard III, Hamlet, Othello, Lear, Coriolanus, and some lesser but rewarding roles like Sir Giles Overreach in Massinger's *A New Way to Pay Old Debts*. He was received better in some than in others, but he became the darling of Drury, of London, of Britain. (There is still today a Kean Street off Drury Lane.) By 1816 a London newspaper said that Englishmen had stopped talking about the weather when they met in the street; instead they asked each other what they thought of Kean's Giles Overreach.

But the marks of his struggle, his chancy boyhood and youth, had not been erased. He drank, he gambled, he roistered. His marriage, which had never been good, grew worse now that poverty did not chain the pair together. Perhaps worst of all was his realization that not even reaching the pinnacle of his profession would bring him social acceptance. In the theatre he was imperial; in a ballroom, to which he might have been invited as an amusing curiosity, he was, as the law once put it, a rogue and vagabond. This was an abnormally sensitive man of whom it was said that he could see a sneer across Salisbury Plain. To live in a stratified society and be treated as a lackey by his intellectual and spiritual inferiors was a very hot and real hell for Kean.

He did not lack for praise. Byron, who was much involved in the affairs of Drury Lane, was overwhelmed by him. After he saw Kean for the first time Byron wrote in his journal: "By Jove he is a soul! Life—nature—truth without exaggeration or diminution." Kean's sister-in-law wrote to a friend: "Lord Biron [*sic*] is enchanted with Edmund and is like a little dog behind the scenes, following him everywhere." Byron presented gifts to Kean—a Turkish sword and a snuffbox—and addressed a poem to him which began:

> *Thou art the sun's bright child!*
> *The genius that irradiates thy mind*
> *Caught all its purity and light from heaven.*

Coleridge provided the most frequently quoted line on the subject: "To see Kean act is like reading Shakespeare by flashes of lightning." Shelley intended Kean to play the Count in *The Cenci*. Keats, who said, "One of my ambitions is to make as great a revolution in modern dramatic writing as Kean has done in acting," wrote his one finished play, *Otho the Great*, for him. (The actor, with good theatrical

sense, however, never played in either Shelley's or Keats's literary drama.)

But Kean did not lack for trouble, either. His hurricane temper, occasional drunkenness, and illness brought him into conflict with managers. His personal life seethed until it erupted in a suit by one Alderman Cox against Kean for "criminal conversation" with Mrs. Cox. Kean and Mrs. Cox had, in fact, been lovers for some years. That she was a rather permissive lady and that her husband had probably known this, were considered irrelevant. After a newspaper orgy of scandalous articles and cartoons, the alderman was awarded £800 damages.

Professional and personal troubles combined on the night in January, 1825, when Kean returned to the stage after the alderman's victory. The house was packed and hostile; the audience kept up a storm of hooting and abuse, punctuated with orange peels, so that although he played out the entire role of Richard III, not one word was heard. He continued to fight back night after night, insisting on playing and delivering curtain speeches, but he made little headway against the hostility and decided to give the ostentatious moral outrage time to subside while he toured America.

He had made one previous American tour in 1820, when he had been only the second London star to visit this country. His predecessor was George Frederick Cooke, who died in New York and was buried in St. Paul's Churchyard, where a monument to him was erected by Kean. New York, Boston, Philadelphia, and Baltimore had welcomed Kean, but on his return trip to Boston he incensed an audience by refusing to play because there were too few people in the house. The action was inexcusable, and there was no reason now for Kean to expect anything but the rude reception he unmistakably got when he went back to Boston a third time. Yet other American cities, as far south as Charleston, hailed him and restored his finances and confidence. On this tour he also acted in Montreal and Quebec, and in Canada was made an Indian chief, perhaps the first visiting European celebrity to receive this honor. He was much struck by the ceremony. Later he had a portrait painted in his chief's costume, and used often to put on headdress and buckskin when the firewater was in him.

After more than a year's absence he returned to England to find that the public had forgiven him. The *Times* of January 9, 1827, reported: "When the curtain rose, a general cry of 'Kean! Kean!' resounded from every part of the densely crowded house." But his health, ravaged by drink, work, and temperament, was declining. He had frequently to cancel engagements, he could not learn new plays, and sometimes he even "went up" in old parts. Still he blazed, fitfully but forcefully, up and down Britain and on his one professional visit to Paris. He wrote his estranged wife a pitiful appeal for reunion, which she ignored. He was, however, reconciled with his son Charles and to Charles's choice of acting as a career.

Indeed, his last appearance was with his son. On March 25, 1833, he was announced for Othello at Covent Garden with Charles as Iago. He got as far as the scene in which he cried: "Othello's occupation's gone." (Even collapse knew its cue in Kean's life.) Then he became ill, and then unconscious. He was put to bed in a nearby tavern and a few days later was moved to his house in Richmond. He died there in May, aged forty-three. In another room of the house lay his battered old harridan of a mother, to whom he had recently given shelter. She died twelve days later.

The force of his art became a standard by which other performers were measured. Writing of the tragedian William Charles Macready, Leigh Hunt said: "It is to be recollected that Mr. Kean first gave the living stage that example of a natural style of acting, on which Mr. Macready has founded his new rank in the theatrical world." To the theatre Kean brought a burning, intense style in contrast to the large Handelian classical manner of the school of John Philip Kemble. Beyond this he had an extraordinary effect for an actor: he was a stimulus to the finest artistic minds of his time. He was for them the embodiment in the theatre of romanticism—that movement in which art tried to attain universals through the closely examined adventures of the individual soul. To contemporary poets and visionaries Kean's acting was, in Hazlitt's phrase, "an anarchy of the passions," a revolution for which they hungered and which he demonstrably abetted.

As late as 1898 Kean's reputation was still potent enough to serve as a dramaturgic instrument. In Pinero's *Trelawny of the "Wells,"* aristocratic Sir William Gower objects to his grandson's engagement to an actress. To him, actors are mere gypsies. Then Sir William learns that the girl's mother played with Kean, whom he himself had seen years before; and in the line that changes his attitude and the temper of the play, Sir William says: "Kean! . . . Ah, he was a *splendid* gypsy!"

In the musical play *Kean* Peter Stone, the librettist, and Alfred Drake, the star, presented a Kean whose antecedents were recognizable but whose direct descent was from a different source. Messrs. Stone and Drake, if they were not completely consistent with historical facts, certainly kept faith with the "stage" Kean, as he has been represented for a hundred and twenty-five years in the work that was the basis of their show: a play by Alexandre Dumas *père*, lately revised by Jean-Paul Sartre.

Mr. Drake's production, like Dumas's play, told the story of Kean, the "King of London," in the early nineteenth century, a reigning actor dear to the crowd not only because of his talent but because he has made his way up from their midst. He is in love with a countess, the wife of the Danish ambassador, and is himself pursued by Miss Danby, a stage-

Praise from the Prince of Critics

In going to see Mr. Kean in any new character, we do not go in the expectation of seeing either a perfect actor or perfect acting; because this is what we have not yet seen, either in him or in anyone else. But we go to see (what he never disappoints us in) great spirit, ingenuity, and originality given to the text in general, and an energy and depth of passion given to certain scenes and passages, which we should in vain look for from any other actor on the stage. In every character that he has played, in Shylock, in Richard, in Hamlet, in Othello, in Iago, in Luke, and in Macbeth, there has been either a dazzling repetition of master-strokes of art and nature, or if at any time (from a want of physical adaptation, or sometimes of just conception of the character) the interest has flagged for a considerable interval, the deficiency has always been redeemed by some collected and overpowering display of energy or pathos, which electrified at the moment, and left a lasting impression on the mind afterwards. Such, for instance, were the murder-scene in *Macbeth*, the third act of his Othello, the interview with Ophelia in *Hamlet*, and, lastly, the scene with Friar Lawrence, and the death-scene in Romeo.

—*William Hazlitt, in* Champion, *January 8, 1815*

Mr. Kean is all effort, all violence, all extreme passion; he is possessed with a fury, a demon that leaves him no repose, no time for thought, or room for imagination. He perhaps screws himself up to as intense a degree of feeling as Mrs. Siddons, strikes home with as sure and as hard a blow as she did, but he does this by straining every nerve, and winding up every faculty to this single point alone; and as he does it by an effort himself, the spectator follows him by an effort also. Our sympathy in a manner ceases with the actual impression, and does not leave the same grand and permanent image of itself behind. The Othello furnishes almost the only exception to these remarks. The solemn and beautiful manner in which he pronounces the farewell soliloquy is worth all gladiatorship and pantomime in the world.

—*Hazlitt, in the* London Magazine, *January, 1820*

Three actors play Kean in three different tongues: Georg Reimer (above left) in a German version of Dumas's Kean; Charles F. Coghlan (above right) in his own adaptation of the Dumas play, which he starred in during the 1897 season in New York; and Pierre Brasseur (below) with Marie Ollivier in the French version written for him by Jean-Paul Sartre.

struck young heiress. The Prince of Wales, a friend of Kean's, asks him to give up the Countess to avoid an international incident. Kean suspects that the reason for the request is that the Prince wants to woo her. On stage with Miss Danby, he sees the Prince and the Countess together in the royal box, breaks out of his part (Othello), and insults the Prince. In a final scene, where the Count visits Kean's house, Miss Danby comes out of a bedroom at the last moment to draw suspicion away from the Countess who is hiding in another room. Kean is forgiven by the Prince, is reconciled to Miss Danby, and all ends with a Gallic shrug that accepts the pleasantly inevitable.

Thus the musical comedy, and thus in essence the play by Alexandre Dumas, first presented in 1836. The history of that play has nearly as many twists as the plot itself.

The first twist is that Dumas didn't write it himself—not completely, at any rate. Edmund Kean played in Paris for the first and last time in 1828, and shortly thereafter two busy French playsmiths devoted a total of five days to writing a play about him. Their names were Frédéric de Courcy and Marie Emmanuel Guillaume Marguerite Théaulon de Lambert—the latter gentleman mercifully called Théaulon for short. The play languished unproduced, perhaps because its subject was still alive. Three years after Kean's death the manuscript was brought to Dumas, who was rapidly becoming the most popular dramatist in France. On April 30, 1836, a Dumas play, *Don Juan de Maraña,* was produced in Paris and failed. It was doubtless inconceivable to that fat literary fountain that the theatrical year could proceed without another play of his, so he took over the Théaulon-De Courcy work—probably at the suggestion of Frédérick Lemaître, the great actor, who wanted to play Kean—and altered it to suit Lemaître and himself. Théaulon and De Courcy disappeared from the title page of the play.

Jean-Paul Sartre, a later "collaborator" of Dumas's, asks: "What's Alexandre Dumas's part in this story? I suppose we'll never know. What's sure is that he signed the play and was paid for it." However, in his memoirs Dumas refers to "Kean's terrible glance in Othello," so it seems likely that he saw Kean act, was moved by him, and had more than grist-to-the-mill interest in him as a subject. *Kean, ou désordre et génie* was produced at the Théâtre des Variétés on August 31, 1836, just four months after the previous Dumas play, and was a great success for author and actor. Lemaître felt so proprietary about the work that when another actor presumed to play it some years later, he plastered Paris with signed posters stating: "I am the only *real* Kean."

The play was subsequently translated into German, Italian, Spanish, Portuguese, and Danish, and continued to be played in French; Lucien Guitry performed it in the nineties. In Germany it was a particular favorite, and the late Albert Bassermann was among those well known for portrayals of Kean. When the lurid Ermete Novelli toured America in 1907, the play, in Italian, was a staple in his repertoire.

It was performed in English in New York in the mid-nineteenth century, but its most successful English adaptation was made for his own use by Charles Coghlan, the British-American actor-manager, and first presented in New York in December, 1897. For an unaccountable reason he called the adaptation *The Royal Box* and, even less accountably, changed the names of all the characters. Kean himself became James Clarence, and the reviewers were kept busy exercising their parentheses. "In this scene we see James Clarence (that is, Kean) . . ."

Coghlan had success with *The Royal Box* and two years later was on tour with it when he died in Galveston, Texas. In full fustian fig, the Coghlan version was revived in New York as late as 1928 by the road star Walker Whiteside, and even in those speak-easy days, it managed to run thirty-nine performances.

Dumas's play has twice been filmed. The first, silent, version was made by Russian *émigrés* in Paris in 1922, was directed by Alexander Volkov, and starred Ivan Mozhukhin. The second version was made in Italy after World War II with Vittorio Gassman. The former film is by far the better known. When William Whitebait, the eminent film critic of the London *New Statesman,* retired recently, he wrote a valedictory article in which he remembered, among the highlights of his youth, that "the audience at the Studio des Ursulines so bravoed Mozhukhin in *Kean* that the film had to be stopped and the passage replayed."

As Lemaître induced Dumas to revise the Théaulon-De Courcy script, so in 1953 another actor persuaded Jean-Paul Sartre to revise Dumas. The eloquent Pierre Brasseur had played the role of Lemaître in Carné's film *Les Enfants du Paradis,* and this led him to consider reviving one of that actor's roles. The old play needed refurbishing, and Sartre agreed to do it, partially out of admiration for Brasseur, possibly partly as pure theatrical *jeu d'esprit* One could attribute all kinds of "existential" characteristics to Kean as a Sartrean character: a man outside society seeking to engage with it; a man hovering between realities, aware that the adulation he receives is paid to the less real of his selves; a man tormented by internal conflict into a keener awareness of the anguish of existence. It would not be difficult to make a Sartrean case for *Charley's Aunt.* Sartre himself claims little more than that he "scraped off a bit of rust and mildew." In so doing he provided Brasseur with an excellent vehicle.

The authors of the recent *Kean* were not the first ones to consider the musical use of Dumas's play. On April 18, 1850, Giuseppe Verdi wrote to the manager of the Teatro la Fenice in Venice: "Tell Piave [the librettist], in order to spare time, that if he hasn't been able to find the Spanish drama I indicated, I suggest *Kean,* one of Dumas's best dramas. So many fine things can be done with this play without losing time. I could begin work in a month." The Spanish drama referred to was Gutierrez's *El Trobador.* Piave may not have found it; but another librettist, Cammarano, did. It became *Il Trovatore,* and the subject of *Kean* never, alas, rose with Verdi again.

The Broadway musical version, adapted by Peter Stone from Sartre and hung with songs by Robert Wright and George Forrest, satisfied what might be called a Kean tradition. Actors were responsible for initiating the first two adaptations, and the new one came about at the instigation of Alfred Drake, who drew up the first scenario for this production.

From Dumas to Stone the play has never claimed to be biography; it diverges in several respects from the facts. The play's hero is not married, presumably because Dumas thought his audience would have less sympathy for the torments-in-love of a married man. Kean was not in life an intimate of the Prince Regent; his only recorded contact with the Prince was the gift of a royal purse of one hundred guineas, as a mark of favor, shortly after his Drury debut. The Prince put his box at the disposal of the king of Prussia and the emperor of Russia so that they might see Kean play Othello, but there is no proof that he and Kean ever met. The play's hero is a conscious self-dramatizer, a French mixture of Schnitzler's Anatol, Mozart's Don Giovanni, Leoncavallo's Canio, with a soupçon of Byron. The real Kean, although his actions often superficially resembled those of the fictional one, was the protagonist of a tragedy, not a romantic melodrama. He juggled his assignations, boozed with his cronies, insulted his audiences as the fictional Kean does, but unlike the play, there was never a hint in all this of light-heartedness, of true gaiety. It is the frenzy of a man none the less sentenced for being self-sentenced. Among his papers was found an introspective poem with the lines:

> *Whipt in his childhood, in manhood trained,*
> *In all the vices which the fallen strained.*

The jigging London urchin and the starveling provincial player—even the illustrious international star—could never in remotest fantasy have imagined that some of his life would be acted after him "in states unborn and accents yet unknown." But this theatrical genius has indeed found popular immortality in a colorful melodrama. Kean's sense of humor was limited and bitter; still he might have enjoyed this irony.

Stanley Kauffmann, the film critic of The New Republic, *has written novels and plays (including one about Kean), and was a founding member of the New York Kean Club.*

PARIS
PRESERVED

A Portfolio By RONALD SEARLE

Ronald Searle draws with a pen dipped in a half-and-half mixture of sentiment and satire, of accuracy and absurdity. He loves and he teases. His lines curve as caressingly around the thigh of a Parisian damsel as around the bulbous nose and jowls of her slightly befuddled admirer. The people in his pictures seem always to be poised on the edge of self-revelation, eyes heavy-lidded and half-open, as though behind their superb self-assurance they expect any moment to be surprised in the knowledge that what they are doing is perfectly ridiculous.

Searle himself need have no such doubts. Born in Cambridge, England, in 1920, he studied art there and published his first drawings at the age of fifteen. During World War II he fought in the Far East, where he was captured by the Japanese. Even before his release from the army he was a welcome contributor to many British publications, and since then he has become familiar to American audiences as well —especially for his creation of those horrendous young females, the belles of St. Trinian's, and their male counterparts, the ink-begrimed delinquents of *Down with Skool.* In 1956 he joined the staff of *Punch,* for which he illustrated Alex Atkinson's imaginary travelogues of countries never visited by their author.

Searle's Paris, to be sure, begins in reality. He has been there. Indeed he has published *A Paris Sketchbook,* which is literal and affectionate down to the last *bouquiniste* and *brasserie.* But the Paris that emerges from the HORIZON portfolio on the following pages has been transmuted, passing through the mind of Searle the parodist, from the Paris that is into the Paris that would be if it could. (It will form a part of *Which Way Did He Go?,* to be published next fall by World Publishing Company.) The stones sit in the same place, the horse-meat market is still on the Ile St. Louis, but the lens has gone slightly askew and now refracts a city seen only in Searle's interior eye, a studied singularity that is sometimes more true than the truth.

SIC SEMPER BRITTANIA

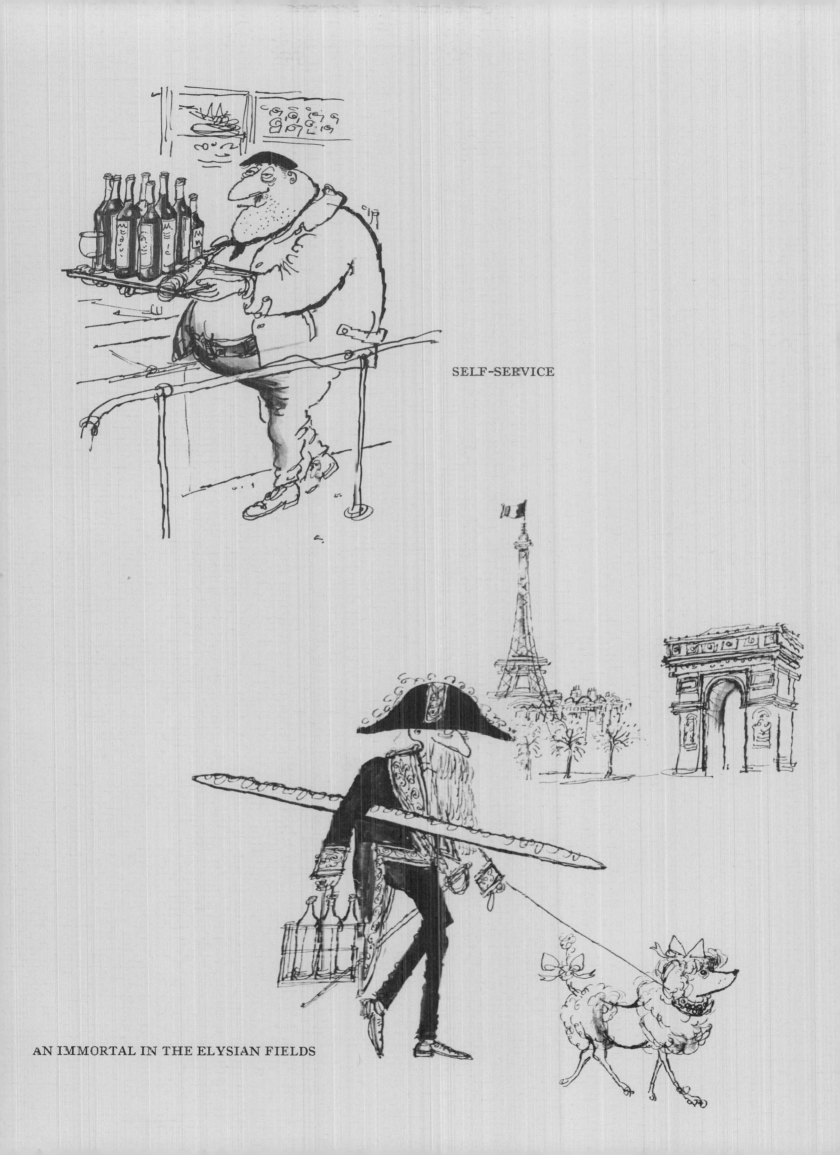

SELF-SERVICE

AN IMMORTAL IN THE ELYSIAN FIELDS

SOME NOTES ON A NATIONAL PASTIME

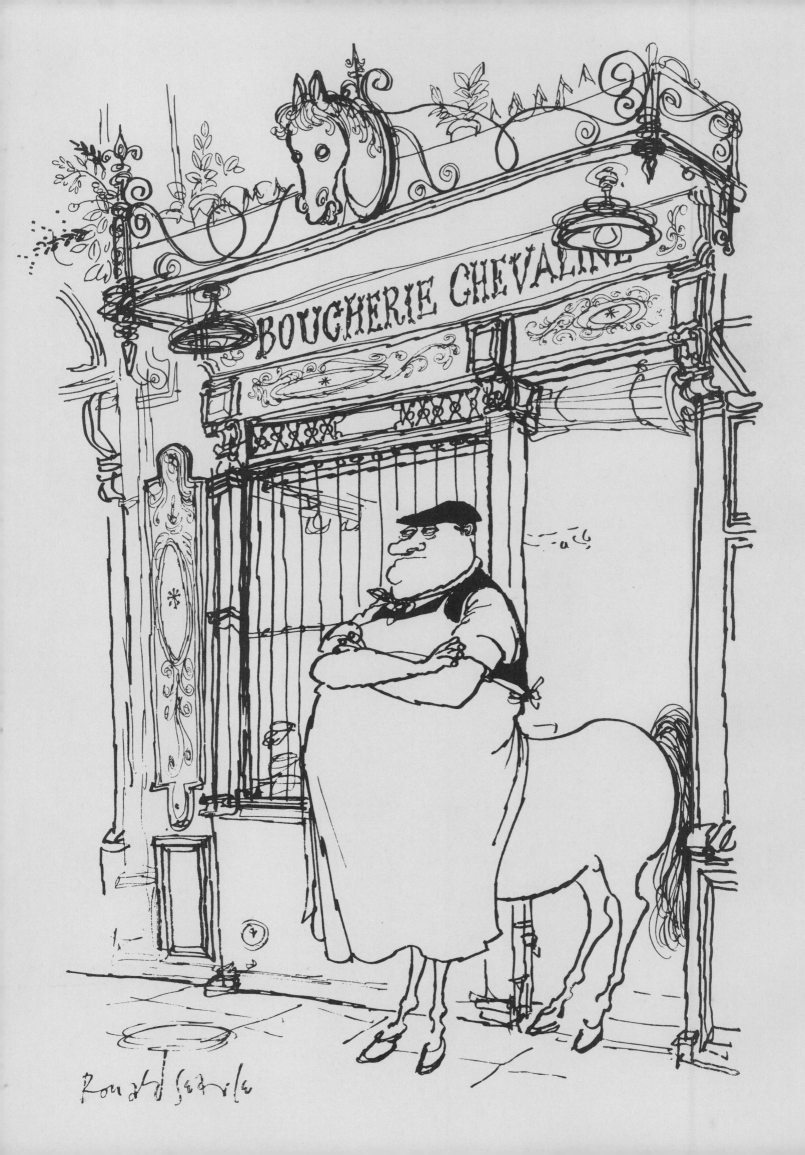